A Dog Behaviourist's Diary

Denise Mcleod

A
Dog
Behaviourist's
Diary

Denise McLeod

Matador
9 Priory Business Park,
Wistow Road, Kibworth Beauchamp,
Leicestershire. LE8 0RX
Tel: 0116 279 2299
Email: books@troubador.co.uk
Web: www.troubador.co.uk/matador
Twitter: @matadorbooks

ISBN 978 1785898 679

British Library Cataloguing in Publication Data.
A catalogue record for this book is available from the British Library.

Printed and bound in the UK by TJ International, Padstow, Cornwall
Typeset in 11pt Aldine401 BT by Troubador Publishing Ltd, Leicester, UK

Matador is an imprint of Troubador Publishing Ltd

I dedicate this book in the memory of my beloved Cassie, Lace, Cloud and Mirk, who inspired it and live on, for all time, within it. I love and miss you all.

Contents

Introduction

Hello and welcome to the book. I hope that you enjoy it.

We all have a story to tell. Each of us has a life which has had trials and tribulations. Sometimes massive ones, and sometimes not. Dogs' lives are much the same. This book tells the stories of some of the lives, trials and tribulations that I have encountered both as a dog owner and a dog-training professional.

This book contains stories that are borne of my actual experience with dog behaviour cases and their owners, or puppies and dogs that have attended class and their owners, or about significant events in my own dog-owning history. There are stories of life and its joys, and sadly of death and its angst and of everything else in between. Wherever possible permission from the case and class clients has been sought to use this information, but in the interest of client confidentiality, all of the names (except Linda, Sabre and Simon) have been changed as well as some of the identifying details.

However, the behaviour issues are presented as they were presented to me and all of the solutions, non-solutions, or processes or events pertaining to dog training or behaviour are as written. They are behaviourally accurate. These are (or were) real dogs and real owners.

Since CaDeLac's inception, we have adhered to our mission statement in all our work: to provide education and help keep dogs in happy, educated, lifelong homes, thereby doing our bit to reduce the numbers of dogs being rehomed or destroyed. The rehoming situation in the UK and elsewhere in the world is at crisis point. There simply are not enough homes or rescue centre places for all the dogs that exist. Every day around the world thousands of dogs are put to sleep for a variety of reasons. There are simply too many dogs than homes, that is for sure, but also there are many dogs who display behaviour that is unacceptable in pets. These dogs find themselves being rehomed, being placed in rehoming centres or occasionally, very sadly, being put to sleep.

I hope that within this book, many people will find new understanding of their dog that will help them resolve, or even avoid altogether, some of the more common behaviour problems.

A bit about me. As a child I was not able to have a dog because of a family illness, so I took it upon myself to find other ways of spending most of my formative moments around dogs, horses, farm animals and wild animals. I spent most of my waking time with animals, watching them, sitting with them, befriending them, training them, raising them, or helping them in some way. I began training other people's dogs, on a hobby basis, in 1992 and in January 2001 I quit my former career to start CaDeLac dog training and behaviour. The name 'CaDeLac' comes from Cassie, the first dog I owned; my name, Denise; and Lace, the second dog I owned. Since that time CaDeLac has been my sole income, and that in itself has been quite an extraordinary adventure!

Over the years CaDeLac has seen over ten thousand puppies and dogs and hundreds of behaviour cases come through its doors. Some of those animals and owners learn what they want and then move on in their lives. Yet others spend many years training with us, progressing through the various levels of expertise, and we witness and hear of their various fortunes, misfortunes, medical issues, behavioural changes, intellectual development, and illness and sadly deaths. And it is that experience that I offer here to you.

Whilst I have spent much of my life learning about dogs in a myriad of ways, spending time with other dog-training professionals, watching endless nature documentaries, reading hundreds of books, watching DVDs and attending dozens of dog-training events, it is from the dogs themselves that I have learnt the most. And it is the learning that I have received from those dogs and people that I share with you here.

Every case is different. Every dog is different. Every owner is different. Every combination of dog, owner, life experience, surrounding influences, urgency, severity, and outcome is utterly unique. Throughout this book I offer my knowledge and approach at the time the event occurred.

I do not profess to 'know it all' about dogs and I am quite sure that as I learn more, my views will evolve and develop as they always have. But I hope that in that which I now share you will find greater understanding of dogs and their people, in addition to humour, joy, as well as frustration and, the inevitable sadness that so often accompanies a life loving and working with animals.

I hope that you enjoy reading the book, and that you will laugh, smile and even cry, on the way.

We have a saying at CaDeLac, which is used often. "Learn and grow, mate. Learn and grow." Nothing could sum up the life of a dog trainer more than those words.

Sit back and have a cup of tea, or a beer. And let me tell you first of all the incredible story of Zak...

A Dog Called Zak

When the call came in I learnt that Zak, a small black crossbreed dog, had apparently begun what sounded like rather extreme, fearful behaviour around his home, and around his owner as well as her two adult daughters and other people. He had not been like this before, but a few months ago, apparently out of the blue, he had started this worrisome behaviour and nothing they had tried could stop him. He was off his food and all he wanted to do was lie in his bed and look miserable. The vet had been called and could find nothing medically wrong with Zak. Preliminary phone questioning gave little away and I made the decision to see this dog as soon as I possibly could.

These days I try to do consultations in my consult premises if I can, but back then in my early days I didn't have that luxury, so most private consults were done in the owner's home. A sometimes perilous business, but I will come to that in another case! There are definitely some cases, and this was one of them, that *need* to take place in the owner's home, if that is where the dog's behaviour is at its worst, as was the case here.

Idiopathic fear is fear without an apparent cause. Usually there is something, but in the preliminary enquiries nothing presented itself. I was clueless as to what I was going to find, so as per usual I was mulling over possibilities in my mind as

1

I drove toward the house a few days later, and coming up with very few ideas.

On arrival I could see that the house was a large, well built, semi-detached residence in a nice semi-rural setting, opposite a big park that until recently Zak had apparently enjoyed so much. The garden was neat and when the door was answered I was presented with a well-dressed, kindly, but tired and sad-looking older lady. As we dealt with the formalities of greetings and I removed my shoes, as seemed to be the way in this home, I recognised the smell of slight damp in the house. I remember searching for clues in the environment as I had found none in the phone call and I really wasn't sure what I was looking for here. I noted that the house had some curtains shut, which seemed odd to me on a sunny day. I noticed also that the house 'felt' a little sad. Some houses do. Some people do. But beyond that, it was large, spacious and well kept.

Working in dog behaviour is a bit like being a detective, I suppose. You are constantly looking around for clues as to the cause, as knowing the cause, though not always possible, will certainly help when conjuring up a solution. In most cases, delving through a dog's history will uncover starting points for behaviours; relevant incidents, experiences, illnesses, or other things which can affect a dog's behaviour. Sometimes, undesirable behaviour starts suddenly, as this case apparently had. Other times there is a gradual increase in the momentum or extent of a behaviour. But in nearly every case I have seen there is a clue of some sort in the history of the dog.

As we chatted briefly on the doorstep, I noticed something missing from the usual scene of 'dog behaviourist arriving at dog's house'. Barking. There was no barking. Indeed, there was no dog!

We entered the house and wandered up the long corridor toward the bottom of the staircase, and she explained that they were living mainly in an upstairs room these days – the views were better from there. We trundled along the dimly lit corridor to the foot of the stairs and the owner signalled politely for me to go first. As soon as I mounted the first step I could see Zak, above me, in a doorway at the top of the stairs. His hackles seemed to be raised and he looked stiff, concerned, frightened, anxious; but strangely almost semi-welcoming. He kind of pleaded with me with his eyes. I felt as if he was trying to telepathically communicate his troubles to me. But if he was, I couldn't understand them. As I looked at him and he watched me ascend the stairs toward him, he took a step forward, uttered a low growl, then stepped back and wagged his tail limply, then another step and a growl, and then another step back and a wag. As I got closer, he began to grovel, with a limp but increasingly enthusiastic wag of his sad-looking tail.

There was something very wrong with this dog, and all I knew was that my heart had gone out to him. My advice to anyone in these circumstances would be not to go upstairs toward a growling dog that is standing above you with its hackles raised. Growling usually means 'back off' or 'stop what you are doing', or 'stop approaching', and as a general rule it's usually worth heeding, for safety's sake, the signals that such a dog is giving. But in this case I had no fear of the dog's intent. He didn't feel threatening in any way. It didn't even seem like he was growling at me – maybe at the owner behind me? It was a very confusing set of signals I was receiving and I just couldn't work them out. But I wanted to get closer to him. I couldn't read the signals, they made no sense and so instead I chose to go with my feelings, which were urging me to get closer to understanding this worried little dog and help him as much and as quickly as I could.

If ever any dog looked like he wanted someone to resolve his troubles, it was this one.

Following my standard protocol of not wanting to change anything at all in the dog's world until I understood it more, I did not greet the dog as a person might ordinarily. Instead I smiled at him, nodded politely and walked past, finding a seat and asking if I could sit. I made no effort to approach or touch him, but instead gave him the time to check me out and decide what he wanted to do in this situation that was new to all of us. The quiet lady ushered me to sit and then she left the room to organise a cup of tea.

As she left the room, my attention turned to Zak. He was now back in his bed and was looking at me dolefully. As I had reached the top of the stairs he had turned away from me and skulked off in slow motion to his bed to one side of the room, where he lay stiffly and sadly. As I glanced at him briefly, now lying in his bed, he held my gaze for a few moments before averting his gaze. I looked away and from the corner of my eye I saw him looking back at me. He was staring intently, but with what looked like pleading in his eyes, and as I looked back at him, he did the same as before: he held my gaze briefly then looked away.

Hmm. Something was very wrong with this dog. I could feel it in every inch of my body. But what was wrong?

The lady owner returned with the tea and we set off trying to discover what had brought about the dog's change of behaviour.

I learnt that Zak had occasionally in the past had upset moments. He got worried if babies cried nearby him, he didn't like shouting and would be concerned if children were screaming and shouting outside his home. But these worried moments had been just looks of concern or a general quietening of his behaviour. It wasn't until recently that they had become prolonged. Oddly, she mentioned that he also got upset if he heard someone being physically sick.

Now back in those very early days of my career I was mostly good with dogs, but less so with people. When people said odd things I just thought, *what an odd thing to say*, and left it at that. But these days with so much more experience of people and cases and taking case history notes, I always enquire further when people say odd things. The question I should have asked was, "What makes you say he doesn't like the sound of people being sick?" But I didn't, and so I continued with my questions.

The basic problems that I was asked to resolve were Zak's apparent disinterest in food; the fact that he no longer went downstairs to the door when people came; that he no longer barked excitedly at people who visited; and that he would, if dragged, still go out for a walk, and on a walk he did seem brighter, but as soon as they turned to come home he would pull back, not wanting to go near the house. Zak was about seven years old and the behaviour had started around six months previously. Prior to this, apart from being mildly nervy in some circumstances Zak had been a relatively happy dog; loving walks, excitedly greeting people at the door, very friendly with family and strangers, loved to play ball, loved to eat, run and play.

This type of sudden onset extreme personality shift is usually the result of a terrible shock or illness, in my experience. Dogs who have been involved in traffic accidents spring to mind as the sort who might suddenly display this type of dramatic, fairly global change.

My questioning continued. Had anything changed in the house? Had there been any building work done? (Building work accounts for soooooooo many different behaviour cases!) Had there been any emotional upset? Family trauma? Arguments? People moving in or out? Any roadworks outside? Bad thunderstorms? Loud noises? Drunk people?

Loud parties? Crying babies nearby? Problems with other dogs? Illness of the dog? A car accident? Illness in the owner, or in her two daughters? Had there been noisy radiator pipes? A noisy cistern? Foxes in the garden? Car accidents outside? Fires? Floods? Earthquakes? I was getting desperate. Anything at all unusual?

No, she replied. There had not.

Nothing. I had *nothing at all* to go on.

So unable to identify a cause, and feeling more helpless and sad with each passing moment, looking at her worried, tormented dog, I wondered if there had been any cruelty; any beatings. She didn't look the sort, yet I had seen no affection between them, as such.

I asked her to call her dog toward her from his bed. He acknowledged his name immediately, his ears flicked further back and there was a flip at the end of his tail, but he didn't move toward his owner.

I encouraged her to try harder, and slowly, reluctantly, the little black dog got up from his bed and with his ears pinned back, his tail curled between his legs and slight rounding of his back, he tiptoed toward her and when he arrived he turned his back to her and sat down at her side. She stroked his head, and he looked anxious.

She hugged him and placed a kiss on his head, and a tear rolled from her eye. She looked up at me and I moved uncomfortably as she looked at me, tears and pleading in her eyes as she begged me again.

"Please, please, make my Zakky happy again."

Zak sat there, immobile. Uncomfortable. Worried. She stroked him and he obliged by sitting still. He occasionally wagged his tail, but he looked so upset. He looked at me and again I felt as if he was trying to tell me something, then he looked away and stared at the wall. She too looked at me, then looked away. There was something that they both knew that I didn't, of that I was sure. But nothing I asked revealed anything.

So with nothing to go on other than that both dog and owner were very unhappy about the other, I set about treating symptoms blindly. I felt a useless fraud. Something was clearly very wrong and I just couldn't work it out.

Over the years I have come to follow a very simple philosophy about making life better, and in cases like these, I apply it to dogs too: *Whatever you love, do that.*

So, as with any dog suffering some kind of fearful or depressive or worried, anxiety-riddled state, or indeed where it has been ill and needs building up mentally, work out what your dog likes and do more of it, as long as there are no medical counter-indications and as long as what the dog likes to do is not in itself harmful or dangerous. So no sky diving for dogs! For some dogs this could be playing more ball games, or swimming, or using their nose to track down bits of food or their toys, or running freely with the dogs they are best friends with. For others it is learning to do new things: tricks, obedience, agility. Anything that the dogs love. In simple terms, when a mind is in turmoil, switch on the happy side of the brain and in so doing, you can effectively diminish the power of the turmoil, anxiety or fear.

So with so little to go on I offered what recommendations I could. Things I knew might help.

Zak liked long walks and chasing balls, but the owner hadn't felt like driving anywhere with him as he had seemed so worried. She had unwittingly reduced his pleasurable outings.

I increased them. He wasn't scared in the car so that was a good time for him, as well as the walks at the end.

He had apparently lost a lot of weight and was clearly below a healthy weight, because he had not been eating properly, so we changed his diet to something more nourishing and palatable and we added tiny amounts of cheese to it every day for a short while, with liver and steak on occasion too. We introduced new toys that he had never encountered, interactive toys to work his brain. And we decided to bring my dogs for a walk the following day so he had friendly, confident company.

I advised she use the predecessor of the now commonly known ThunderShirt, a tight child's tee shirt, to see if that brought him comfort.

I advised a sheepskin rug in his bed, as I've never found a dog or person yet who doesn't love the feel of a sheepskin rug.

We placed cut dry lavender around all the rooms he had access to. Lavender is thought to make one feel more relaxed and promote good sleep.

We added homeopathic drops to his daily water, to calm him.

We changed his water from tap water to bottled water, and as money was not an issue, we tried different types of bottled water to see which one he preferred. I have always wondered what tap water does to some dogs, and I often find that bottled water for a while can bring about positive results so it's always worth a shot!

I could see a look of hope beginning to creep across his owner's face. Her shoulders, which had been slumped, raised slightly, and she said, almost like a lost child, "And do you think that that will make Zak better?" There was a glint in her eye.

I hadn't any idea whether it would or not but it would buy me time, time to think, to call my behavioural friends, my vet, my first instructor and my third instructor– the ones most likely to be able to help me– and a couple of experienced allies to see what they thought. And it was going to bring the lady hope and hope can be really powerful, and it was a change. Sometimes a change – any change – works.

As I was preparing to leave I had a sudden thought that I

should quickly take Zak out alone on the lead. She said that was fine. I wondered if I could suss anything out when I had him alone on a walk. I put his lead on and he got up cautiously to come with me. He got to the door and tensed visibly as I walked toward the top of the stairs. He pulled back slightly on the lead and tension raced up the lead and into me. I felt the rush of anxiety course through me, and then suddenly he raced to my leg and slunk against the wall, as if to get away from something on the other side of me. The whole energy of the situation had shifted, I felt: there was now hope, but suddenly again, fear. We reached the bottom of the stairs and he rounded the corner to face the corridor and front door. Zak's owner was walking cautiously behind us.

As we turned Zak looked up toward the ceiling over the stairs and barked and barked and pulled back away from the point he was barking at. The whites of his eyes flashed and there was fear on his face. I looked at his owner for any sign from her; she had anguish written all over her face. Zak was growling and barking and still backing away, and then suddenly he fled forward, almost as if he was ducking under something. He flew along the corridor toward the front door, taking me with him in his unexpected move. He got to the door, cowered against it, and looked back and forth at me and then the door handle, clearly wanting out. Now.

I recovered my balance after the heady and surprising dash down the corridor and turned to face his owner. She stood at the bottom of the stairs, looking up, transfixed, at the gap above the stairs that Zak had been barking at and then slowly her face crumpled, she let out an enormous, painful, gut-wrenching howl, fell to her knees and began to sob hysterically. There in the hall. I looked at Zak and he looked at me. And I looked at her. She was on her knees, slouched, howling and sobbing. The noise she made cut right through me; it was a howling release and expulsion of emotional pain, interrupted by deep, powerful sobs and then gasps for air.

She had completely fallen apart.

This was one of my earliest cases and was the first time that I had come across such emotion in an owner, and I really didn't know what to do next.

I looked back at Zak. I hoped somehow that he might show me what to do. But he was now looking fixedly at the point between the door and its frame, wishing that he could slide through it like a postage stamp, I felt. But in reality he was shutting down, away from the situation, and things began to become clear to me.

I went to the lady, knowing Zak was rooted safely in his fear. And slowly, after many minutes her sobbing subsided and she started to try to talk.

"My son. Died there." She pointed vaguely to the top of the stairs. "Hung himself," she said simply, and began to sob uncontrollably again. I looked up at the space where her son had died, I looked at Zak and Zak continued to look at the gap he wanted to get through.

"Oh no, oh, I'm so sorry," was all I could think of. How awful for her!

"I feel so ashamed." That was another statement that surprised and saddened me. This case was certainly a turning point for me in so many ways.

Over the next hour or so, she started to tell the story of her son's illness. His depression, and the terrible sickness from the medication. She was deeply religious and she considered that his suicide was a sin, and she felt terrible guilt and torment as well as normal grief and anxiety, which her dog had reacted so badly to. They had become locked in an endless spiral of negative behaviour and thoughts.

Because of the huge guilt she felt, she had spoken to no

one of her son's death. She had not seen a doctor or sought any help. She had kept all her feelings inside except for when she had those sobbing, howling fits, when she usually sought Zak's physical presence, although Zak himself had been avoiding it, making her feel even worse. It was a terrible, horrible situation. And once again, I felt out of my depth.

After more tea, I left. She had calmed and Zak too seemed calmer and had gone back upstairs without barking at 'the space'. So assuring her of my return with my own dogs the next day, I left to consult more experienced people than me and come up with a plan to help this poor lady and her overwhelmed little dog.

I rang all the wise people I could get hold of. The phone calls went on late into the night, but I was not concerned; I knew I wouldn't sleep anyway. I just wanted to share and talk and hear others who might have had such an experience, who had answers. But no one had, it seemed. I rummaged through all my dog books, consulting the wise writers of the time: John Rogerson, Karen Prior, Ian Dunbar. But no one had written of anything similar. So I just stayed awake and thought. And thought. I thought of counter-conditioning Zak to the lady's physical advances. Her outbursts – link them with play? Change the interior of the house, the routine, anything to get them away from their preoccupation with 'that space' above the stairs? But the dog *had* to pass that place to toilet, to walk, to gain pleasure in his life.

The lady too had to confront the memory every day on her way to the outside world, even to the kitchen, or they both lived in the living room, upstairs, indefinitely.

What to do, what to do, what to do?

I hoped that when we walked tomorrow something would come to me.

Sometimes, even often, even now, with all the experience I have gained, the answer is not always as obvious as one might think it ought to be. No matter how many times you encounter fear, aggression, madness, illness, sadness, or unfortunate or misguided habits, in dogs or people, each one remains utterly unique. And as such, the solution, or non-solution, is utterly unique as well. It *has* to be, else it won't work. It has to fit the owner, the dog, the time constraints, the environment, the urgency, the level of danger or risk. It has to be unique, and you have to create it, sometimes, in a hurry. Sometimes it is urgent. This lady and her dog were in a terrible place of neediness but wariness of each other, and neither could resolve it. Every day, literally, their difficulties compounded.

As I arrived the next day with a carload of dogs to cheer Zak up, I still remained clueless as to what to suggest other than what I had already suggested. With trepidation I approached the house. But as the lady answered the door there was a difference in her attitude. She wore a look of expectancy. Of hope. But still sad hope, desperate hope. But I was still clueless.

We got Zak past 'that place' and out into the world. All of my dogs seemed to sense the desperation of the circumstance and my mood, and responded brilliantly, meeting the little dog gently and kindly and surrounding him in an odd way, almost as if they were protecting him.

As we trotted down the road on lead they looked like they were all being older siblings to fearful little Zak. It was heart-warming in the extreme. We let them off lead on the field and my Cassie approached him and succeeded in getting Zak to play. Tears poured down the owner's face as she watched him romp around and get pounced on. My tears followed as I saw her smile for the first time since I'd met her.

We chatted more about her son's death. The sadness

she felt, the confusion, the anger she felt at God, or who or whatever she had formerly believed in. Her former faith was now in complete disarray. The conversation went on and it somehow flowed as the dogs played around us and did dog things.

When we arrived back at the house we had a bit of a hubbub getting Zak and his dear lady back into the sitting room to talk. Tea was once again served. Zak and I studied one another from a gentle distance. My dogs were now lightening the place up a bit, with one stealing things out of the bin, me apologising for their crap behaviour (no doubt she was expecting or hoping that my dogs would at least be reasonably well-behaved dogs!), one still trying to get Zak to play, and a borrowed dog lying down, zonked out, snoring loudly. They were all looking utterly unfazed by 'that space' or anything else that went on. Confidence-givers.

And still nothing had come to me. No more ideas.

She sat down, looking expectantly at me, and I felt obliged to say something, so I did. It seemed outrageous as I said it out loud, but I had thought of it last night and dismissed it as too trite. But I hadn't thought of anything else.

"A holiday." I sounded more confident than I felt. "You and Zak need to get away from this house, at least for now." It was starting to feel right to me. That little green light had come on in my head, saying, *yep, you're on it now...*

"A holiday," I continued, confidently now. "You need to go away from here, to a lovely place, somewhere you love. Do things you love. Whatever you love, do that! Be with people that you love if you know any far away from here. Accept that you are going to feel sad, but feel sad somewhere else. Somewhere beautiful, warm, sunny, happy, neutral. Anywhere but here. Where there is no daily confrontation with the images in your head, the feelings, the history. That place." I gasped as I said it, hoping it would make sense to her.

And as her eyes lightened, I knew that she too knew that a break away was exactly what they both needed.

So off they went. She rang me three weeks later. Zak and she had been up to Scotland to see an old school friend who had written to her, offering her support. Whilst there, Zak had made several friends. She had decided to sell the house without returning to it. A terribly brave move, but one which perhaps, here, was the only option? An extreme solution to a very extreme problem.

This was one of the most important and life-changing cases I ever worked on. And I will write below about the lessons I learnt in that case. Important – no, hugely important lessons that everyone working in dog behaviour should know.

It was a few months before I heard again from Zak's lovely lady owner, and it was unusually late at night when the call came in. 'Unusually late at night' in my world means a probable bite incident or something with police involvement – or worse.

I had thought of Zak and his owner often and wondered how things had gone, but had been strangely scared to call to find out. I'd never seen such a traumatised dog and owner, and too often fear is difficult to resolve satisfactorily.

When I picked up the phone the voice I heard was both familiar and unfamiliar at the same time. She sounded different. There was an immediate jolt in my chest as I heard her voice and I recalled that poor lady sobbing in the hallway, her arm waving toward 'that place' as I saw her dog desperate to escape the situation. Every cell in my body immediately strained to read the tone of the words that were to come in this phone call. I wanted to know immediately if things had worked out well, or not.

It took only a few seconds to know, and I heaved an internal sign of relief.

Zak was doing really well. She was much better too. She would always miss her son of course, and so would Zak, but life in the new house was working well. Zak and she were enjoying lovely daily walks and he was eating well and enjoying life with a number of new doggy friends. She too had found people to be most kindly toward her as they learnt of her situation, and she had been touched and moved that no one had judged her, or her son, at all. Quite the opposite – people had shown enormous kindness and had been a great source of support. She saw people differently these days. She couldn't thank me enough. But I made clear that it was her courage and determination, not mine, that had taken her so far from home to recover.

She had also done a very clever thing, something which I have since adopted as an approach to relieving fear and stress. She had bought Zak a big soft teddy bear, so that he could still have contact with something soft. Many dogs love to sleep on another body. It stems from early puppyhood when they found safety, warmth or comfort in the pile of puppies they were born with. Not all dogs do, but many.

Sadly, she said, Zak and her relationship had not returned completely to the touchy-feely relationship they had had before her son died. He was no longer scared of her, she felt, but he still didn't want to be touched or hugged by her, and occasionally when she looked at him he would growl. Thankfully, miraculously, she had stuck strictly to a very important piece of advice I had given her: I had told her that *under no circumstances* should she *ever* make advances to touch Zak unless Zak had approached her looking as if that was what he wanted. She had found this very hard, she said. All owners do. She had longed to touch him so. But she had heeded my warning that any advancement on Zak could jeopardise progress. I had made it clear that the most important aspect of any recovery in the breakdown of any relationship between dog and owner is that both parties take whatever time and whatever approach they *both* need to recover. If she really wanted to help Zak, she needed to respect that he needed to work things out in his own way, in his own time. Like her, he had been truly traumatised and sometimes time was the only thing that could really heal such a trauma. It was up to him, not her, to decide when *he* was ready to move on.

And that, it transpired, was the very reason she had called me at this moment, so late at night. She couldn't wait to tell me, and thought I *must* be the first person to know. Because right at that moment, Zak was curled up at her side, on the sofa, for the first time since her son had died. Only an hour earlier, for no apparent reason, he had slowly progressed across the room toward her, and cautiously, gently and one paw at a time, he had heaved his tired body up beside her. He had circled, sighed and lay down. His back was resting against her thigh at that very moment as she spoke to me.

I saw it in my head, little Zak, asleep at her side.

That was when the sobs came again, but this time, it was from my end of the phone. From their end, I heard the wonderful sound of true joy in a person's voice, and I'm pretty sure I could hear the equally wonderful sound of a gently snoring dog!

I learned so much from Zak and his owner, and from her son too, and for that I thank them all. Due to them, through that learning, I was able to help other dogs and people in new ways. Clearly I didn't learn enough though, for several years later, after trauma in my own life, I too lost a very special connection with a very special dog, one of my own, because of emotional thunderstorms. But that is another case...

Remember always that whilst some dogs can and do support their owners through emotional trauma – they might lick your hand, snuggle their nose into your ear, lick away your tears, become easier to manage, lie on your bed day and night – to other dogs, emotional outbursts – crying, howling, sobbing, disruption, anything intensely emotional – can be truly traumatic and can utterly destroy a dog's confidence in both their owner and their life. Neither sort of dog is right or wrong, good or bad, just different, and each must be respected for exactly who or what they are. They must be allowed to *be* exactly who or what they are – in their own way and most importantly, in their own time.

Clown: The Dog Who Could See Ghosts

The curious case of the dog that could see ghosts. When the call came in about Clown it sounded very interesting. Apparently, her owner reported, Clown was able to see ghosts. The owner too had once seen a ghost in her house, in her kitchen, and now Clown could see them too and it was clearly upsetting her. The odd behaviour that Clown was displaying was related to just the one room in the house, the kitchen in which the owner had also seen the ghost. I asked who had seen the ghost first and she couldn't remember, but she thought that the first time Clown had seen it and the only time she herself had seen it had been around the same time. This was a case I was looking forward to, so I shifted my caseload about a bit to see this one quickly, and with a lot of interest in my heart I set off the next week. A ghost, no less – how exciting!

When I arrived at the little neat-looking semi I was welcomed in, and Clown appeared to be a balanced, well-mannered dog, in tune with her owner. She was around two years old, had been well reared and socialised and was of a Border Collie cross type. After I arrived, tea was mentioned and as her owner went off into the kitchen, Clown watched her go but made no attempt to follow her. Clown's owner closed the door behind her and the dog lay there, looking at the closed door and then back at me, wagging her tail as I caught her gaze briefly.

When the owner returned with two mugs of tea, she again carefully shut the kitchen door behind her so as not to upset the dog and we got down to examining the facts of the case.

Clown had been a well-loved and affectionate puppy and had shown no signs of any odd behaviour until a few months previously. She had, from time to time, barked at some people whilst out on walks, if they were alone, wearing a hat, or had anything 'odd' about them. The barking was sometimes accompanied by raised hackles. This all sounded pretty normal to me. Most dogs bark at someone during their early years if they are wearing a hat or odd clothing. The owner had thought that hackles raising signified aggression, but Clown had never done anything else aggressive. I explained that raised hackles are indeed *not* necessarily a sign of aggression, merely arousal or excitement, and as Clown had not done anything else it didn't sound aggressive. The owner was clearly relieved.

The problem seemed to be that on occasions, though not always, Clown had shown the same behaviour at the threshold of the kitchen door. Hackles raised, she barked, then took a step forward, then back, barking continuously, then repeated the behaviour. She was clearly upset and distressed, and the owner had not understood. She had looked in the kitchen but could see nothing to upset Clown, and later the same day the dog would go back into the kitchen without being upset. The owner was confused and the behaviour was causing problems because the entrance to the garden was through the kitchen, so sometimes Clown would not pass through to go out to toilet.

This had happened many times. In the daytime, Clown had often barked and raised her hackles and refused to go into the kitchen, but on enquiry it seemed that this had never

happened at night-time, which was odd as I always think of
ghosts as being mainly nocturnal things.

I asked about the ghost that the owner had seen: she had
seen 'something' walk through the kitchen one evening.
Digging deeper, I found that her memory was unclear but
she thought that it had been dark outside and she distinctly
remembered that Clown had *not* shown a fearful reaction that
night, so she obviously didn't see the ghost when the owner
saw it.

How odd.

Now I have seen a few things in my time that I could only
consider as paranormal or ghosts, and my dogs too had reacted
to a ghost once, in my house. That house was old and had been
built on a Roman road. One day I had seen 'something' move
through the house whilst I sat watching TV. Lace had been lying
on the sofa with me, and Cassie lay nearby. Neither dog had
reacted at that moment. But then after about a minute when
the apparition had gone, they had both jumped up, showing
distress and fear, and had fled upstairs together. This was most
odd as they hated one another and rarely did anything together
without fighting about it. So I was not surprised that on the
night when the owner had seen the ghost, her dog hadn't.

What I had noticed about these events was that I often felt a
chill when it happened, and so now, opening the kitchen door
with some trepidation, I stepped into the haunted kitchen. But
there was nothing about the kitchen that unnerved me. It was
warm, bright and cosy. Illuminated by the sun, it shone with
cleanliness and freshness and I could hardly imagine a place
less like a haunted house. Nah, I didn't think there was a ghost
here. If there had been, it wasn't here now.

So my attention turned back to Clown and her owner.
Carefully closing the kitchen door behind me, I asked the
owner if we could see if Clown would go through the kitchen

so I could watch her behaviour. The owner went to the door and called her dog to her. Clown looked a little concerned but obliged. As the owner opened the door, Clown looked and fixated briefly, before, as described, her hackles rose and she alert-barked, taking a step forward then back, not keen on going into the kitchen. Now I don't like unsettling dogs so I didn't like what came next, but I needed to see more of her behaviour so I asked the owner to try to get her through the kitchen to the back door. Clown was still barking and clearly not wanting to go on, but as her owner insisted, Clown made a hurried, scuttling dash for it, veering left along the wall and shooting out the back door like a bullet. Her re-entrance to the room from the garden a few moments later was similar – a headlong dash as she clung to the wall and arrived back in the living room, where she calmed.

I was mystified. But then I remembered something similar in a competition I had entered as a child with my pony. It was called 'Handy Pony' and required that the competitors asked their ponies to do odd things, like walk over a plastic bag, walk through a line of washing, over an unstable surface, close to vehicles, etc. It was designed, I think, to test the trust between horse and rider and was to all intents and purposes a great habituation exercise. My pony had once taken fright at a plastic bag on a pole which he was to pass. So I had got off him to see things from his point of view and it was clear that he couldn't see past the large bag from the angle of approach, so I changed the angle and he calmed.

I remembered too my first agility instructor telling me that if your dog won't tackle an obstacle or is behaving oddly, get down to his level and *see for yourself* what he is seeing, hearing or feeling. So that is what I did: I went to the kitchen door on my hands and knees, which made me about Clown's height, and knelt there on the threshold, to see if from here, there were any ghosts. First I listened. Nothing odd to hear. Then I looked; nothing odd to see. Then I tried to *feel*. Nope. I smelt the air. There was just the smell of cleaning products and freshly laundered washing. At that moment Clown came over and stood next to me, clearly curious as to what I was doing.

She was no longer upset, it seemed; she was quite relaxed, and instead she just looked at me like, *What the heck are you doing?* Then all of a sudden we had a moment of illumination, literally. It was one of those white fluffy cloud days and the sun had been going in and out throughout the consultation, but at that moment when the sun came out Clown's behaviour changed. She uttered a low, deep growl, and presumably feeling more confident with me at her side, took a step forward, fixated ahead. More growls and another pace into the kitchen, and I walked with her, side by side, on my now painful knees, to see what she was fixating on. I can only imagine what we looked like from behind, two backsides, one with a tail, one with jeans on, creeping into the kitchen side by side.

Then suddenly, she alert-barked: high-pitched, rapid, frightened. Only inches away from my head, it nearly burst my eardrum in the process... and she stepped back, leaving me alone in the kitchen, on my hands and knees.

And as I looked, I saw. I was staring straight at the washing machine, in the glass of which I saw my own reflection. An idiot on her hands and knees. And there was the answer. When the sun came out, the light reflected somehow off the glass from the cooker and onto my face, providing enough light to generate a reflection in the washing machine door. It was this that had frightened poor Clown. She had been seeing her own reflection, obscured into a strange, contorted shape by the shape of the glass, and only in daylight and only when the sun was out.

The solution was to open the washing machine door a tad

so the angle of reflection changed and Clown could no longer see herself. We agreed that when the washing machine was switched on and its door had to be kept shut, the door to the kitchen would be kept shut so that Clown was no longer faced with her own reflection which scared her so. Simple, effective and immediate. The owner was thrilled at such an easy, cost-free solution, and I was thrilled with her. A week later a box of Thorntons and some wine arrived at my door, so I was even more pleased, and her owner rang to say that happily, neither Clown nor she, had seen any ghosts since that day. Denise Mcleod: dog trainer, behaviourist and ghost buster!

Lace: "Oh, What a Lovely-Looking Dog!"

In around 1991 I decided to get my second dog and my beautiful Lace, my first Border Collie, came into my life. By now I was competing successfully in agility with Cassie, dog ownership was going well and it had brought me a new hobby, new friends and a whole new way of life which I loved.

So wanting to get another dog that was young enough and fit enough to walk the huge distances that Cassie and I were routinely walking and to perhaps compete in agility, I went looking for a new dog.

I went to see a potential candidate, a stunning-looking animal. With a mostly white face and a black patch over one ear and eye, she was the picture of femininity and sweetness. Her white side had a spattering of little black spots, naughty spots as I came to know them.

Lace paid no heed to me and instead she chased after a ball and the woman's young daughter, who had a flowing, flowery skirt, which appealed to Lace as a tug toy.

There was no history available about Lace other than that her previous owner "couldn't cope". The owner of the shelter advised me that she seemed "a bit nippy", but that she would "probably soon grow out of it". Apart from a rather dull coat, she appeared fit and well so I decided to take her for a walk with Cassie to see if they got on, and go from there. I walked up the street with both dogs and though there was no immediate friendship between them, there were no arguments either.

It took a while for Lace to take any notice of me during that first walk together, but eventually when I sat down on a log she leaned against me, and seeing that as a request for contact, I obliged by stroking her. Lace responded, leaning into me warmly and her fate was sealed. I made up my mind to have her and the three of us went home together.

For the next eighteen years Lace taught me lesson after lesson about dog behaviour. She had issues with many things and together Cassie, Lace and I scoured the country looking for help and ways to work through her various issues, giving me reason to invest thousands of hours in study and contemplation as well as training courses regarding those issues.

It didn't take long for me to work out what "a bit nippy" actually meant.

After two days with me she had bitten two people.

The first day she bit a stranger who, unbeknown to me, had touched her as we passed in the street, creating something of a scene between the woman and me. I was shocked and apologised profusely. Then on the second day, she bit me. We had been out walking and she had chased a rabbit into a bramble bush. When we returned home I had tried to remove some brambles from her belly area, and though she had rolled over obligingly and let me see her tummy, as I pulled out the brambles I had accidently snagged her coat. She whirled round and bit me on the hand. It didn't really hurt, it didn't bruise or break the skin, but I was shocked. I had never been bitten by a dog before and it caught me by surprise, and I shouted at her. She looked equally shocked by my shout and she rolled over again. She never bit me, or looked like she might, again.

Indeed, from that moment on Lace seemed to decide that I was her most favourite thing in the world and she quickly became one of the most committed, loving dogs I've ever had. She was an amazing girl and I miss her dearly – if only they could live forever!

I learnt a great deal from Lace. The first and most important thing that I learned because of her, though, was about people, not dogs.

Knowing next to nothing about people-biters back then, so assuming, wrongly, that she had little experience of people and perhaps needed some more positive social interaction, I decided to take her into a nearby small town the next day, and here the lessons began.

It became very clear that Lace was a dog who other people wanted to touch. Her delicate, pretty features attracted all sorts of attention and within five minutes of being in town I saw a woman approach me with a smile on her face as she looked at and admired Lace.

"What a lovely dog," she said, stopping in front of us, smiling at Lace and blocking our way. "How old is she?"

"Around ten months, they think. I am her second home so I don't know for sure," I replied. I watched for Lace's reaction. Lace was watching the woman.

The fact that she had had to be rehomed brought a pitying look. "Aww, poor thing." And without warning or asking, she leaned forward to stroke her.

Now, as a young child I was told more than once, "If you touch a strange dog, it might bite you and no one will feel sorry for you, because it's your own fault. Never touch a strange dog." So I never did, unless it came to me first or I'd known it a while. When I was four years old I made friends with a girl from my first school and began visiting her house. She had a Jack Russell and her mum said to me, "Don't touch the dog, else it will bite you." So I never did. We were friends for many years but I never touched her dog even though I visited their house often. I always wanted to touch it, but they had said she would bite me, so I didn't. Although I loved dogs and I really did want to stroke her... I was desperate for my own dog, so jealous that my friend had one and I didn't. But even with all that going on, I noted that the Jack Russell also never came to me to be touched, nor did she go to anyone I saw visit that house. In fact she rarely went to her owners to be touched or stroked as I had seen other dogs do.

The smiling woman was blocking our passage and seemingly intent on stroking Lace, who was staring at her with a hard look in her eyes. As soon as I realised that she was planning on touching her I said firmly, "Please don't touch my dog, she isn't always friendly. She might bite you."

Having never experienced this before I expected her to heed my warning, but taking me by complete surprise she continued her reach and replied, "No, no, dogs like me." She leant forward and went to place her hand on top of Lace's head. Though surprised by her decision to ignore my request, I was still fast enough to react in time and as Lace, reading the woman's intention, sprang forward, her mouth open and teeth bared, I quickly halted her launch with the lead. Lace reached the end of her lead and thus fell short of the woman's hand, and snapped her teeth shut in a warning.

The woman reeled back from the leaping dog in horror, fear evident on her face, and looked from Lace, who was now standing back calmly, silently contemplating her victim, to me. Shock evident on her face and in her voice, she said accusingly, "Your dog went to bite me!"

"Yes, I know. I said she might."

"Vicious thing. Vile animal, it wants shooting!" She stomped off.

I was bemused. I had told her Lace wasn't friendly and not to touch her, yet she had ignored my warning and now she was calling my new dog vicious.

I realised that Lace, though pretty and very sweet with me, was different to other dogs I had known before and I needed to understand why she did this, and also how to stop her from doing it.

Back in those days it was all a mystery to me, how dogs like Lace came to be people-biters. But these days I am very much clearer on these things. In Lace's case, as with many other particularly attractive or sweet-looking animals, it is a behaviour that they have come to use in order to prevent strangers touching them.

I don't want strangers touching me, you don't want strangers touching you, none of us want strangers touching our children, and yet the popular view seems to be that *all* dogs should allow *all* strangers to touch them, whenever and however they want. Even if the dog is clearly expressing their wish to not be touched.

If I am walking down the street and as I pass a woman I don't know, she reaches out to me and starts to rub my ears or touch my face or head, I will be very perturbed and possibly quite cross. I will probably shout at her, push her hand away, or maybe in surprise even slap her hand. If she did it repeatedly I would go to the police and tell them. I think anyone would feel it reasonable for me to get cross in that situation.

What about you? If you were walking down the street with your young daughter and a stranger said to you, "Can I touch your daughter, please?", what would you say? What if they began to touch your daughter without even asking? What would you do?

So why do people think it's OK to touch a strange dog, and yet mostly they seem to realise that it is not OK to touch a strange adult or child? When someone is convicted of child molesting, they can go to prison. However, when someone touches a dog without the dog or owner giving permission and the dog reacts to that touch with an aggressive display or bite, then it is the dog, not the human, that is assumed by so many to be at fault. Why?

Over the next few weeks I went from saying, "Please don't touch my dog, she isn't always friendly" to "*No! Stop! Do not touch her! She will bite you!*" through to "*She bites, don't touch!*" very loudly. Mostly this last statement halted people's attempts to touch her, but not always. On occasion, even with that strong statement made, people would still respond with "Oh no, all dogs love me" or "Dogs know which people are dog lovers, she won't bite me."

But she did try to bite them. All of them.

Nowadays, of course, I would realise that the sensible thing to do was to muzzle Lace whilst I worked out what to do, but muzzles back then were a rare thing in my world and I simply didn't think of it. Back then, before 'aggressive dogs' became the subject of media attention and what I consider sometimes the victims of unrealistic expectations, I thought that we could progress OK as long as I could find a way of stopping people from touching her. Lace didn't pursue people to bite them, unless they provoked her somehow, she just didn't want to be touched by strangers – which in my view is a perfectly reasonable desire. I saw it as the people's fault, not Lace's. I still do see it that way. But only because the people don't understand what they are doing, how they're causing issues.

Nowadays it is possible to buy leads and jackets for dogs that say things like *I need space*, or *Please don't touch me*. There is also the brilliant yellow ribbon scheme, which encourages people whose dogs get upset with others in their close space to put a yellow ribbon on the dog or its lead, or have it wear a yellow warning bandana so that other people can know. It has been this way with horses for umpteen years: those that are prone to kicking have red ribbons tied in their tails. But back then, communication to strangers relied upon owners or dogs making it clear.

It was a quandary for me. I had been raised to believe that if a dog bit me it was my own fault. And this is the way I still feel today. With very few exceptions, in my experience to date it is very rare indeed for a dog to bite a person with no provocation. But sadly, there are ever increasing numbers of people-biters being created as a direct result of unwanted attention.

In my view, people-biters are most often created by people who do not realise that the dog is so uncomfortable with contact. Unwittingly, unknowingly, they create the situation, by wrongly believing, or simply blindly hoping, that the dog is friendly.

But just think about it for a moment: imagine your life if almost every time you went into a public place people took it upon themselves to walk directly at you, then reach down from above and stroke you, ruffle your ears or give you a firm bash (pat) on top of the head. No matter what you were doing or where your attention is, strangers keep interrupting you and touching you. Every day. Imagine that you gave them a dirty look, you tried to get away, you stared at them pointedly, you even said (growled), "Back off, leave me alone." But still they came and touched you, smiling as if they were enjoying your suffering. How long would it take for you to lose your temper?

Dogs in the home can become this way with their owners and their families too, if at home they are the subject of unwanted attention. 'Let sleeping dogs lie' is a really valuable idea to be shared. Dogs who bite their owners or family members are often found to have had the same problem that Lace had: People want to touch them, when they don't want the attention. The dog has tried to communicate to their owners that they don't want to be picked up at random intervals, or stroked in that spot or at this time, or when they are tired, asleep, or feeing achy or ill. But their communications have failed to get through to the owners and the dog may then resort to taking things to a new level.

And so it was that I slowly began to learn that dogs that looked lovely, like Lace, were often the repeated subjects of unwanted attention. That people seemed to think that because she looked cute, she was cute. They could just walk up and touch her, send their children over to stroke her, or even one day, to my horror, that they could reach for her collar. In fact 'people aggressive' dogs account for a high proportion of my caseload; aggression caused in exactly the same way as it was with Lace. It's often nice dogs, or otherwise good, well-intentioned owners, trying to do the right thing and not seeing discomfort in their dog early enough. Or if they do see discomfort they do the wrong thing. The worst thing: they try to 'socialise' the dog with people more, even holding a dog still as someone strokes them, the mistake I once made with much-missed Cassie, my very first dog.

A dog's warning process can go through several stages. There are fairly subtle things that people often miss. Changes of pace, often slowing. Or if stationary, freezing the face and/or body, or a stare or a general change of attitude from moving, floppy and relaxed to stiff and stiller, or occasionally more active and frenetic. Most dogs develop greater ability to communicate as they age. As young dogs they might go from this stage straight to a snap or bite with no further signals. As dogs age their range of signals can become clearer or more extensive and they can include a range of pre-attack signals, including snarling, growling, lip-quivering, lunging head or body, air-snapping and then ultimately contact with teeth, most usually on the offending outstretched human limb or part of the body nearest and therefore most threatening to the dog.

From the dog's point of view, all of these signals – slowing, staring, freezing, growling, snarling, air-snapping, or even making a single contact snap and release – are valid and actually very normal communication signals from a dog.

They are attempts by the dog to avoid conflict. By trying to make clear that what you are doing, or about to do, is worrying the dog. This is how dogs talk to one another, how they say, "Stay away." Just like with Lace, she did try to warn them, but if they failed to heed the warning then she would make a single lunge and single minor bite that would shock a person, making them withdraw, but not really hurt them. She never bit down hard or shook a person. She rarely drew blood, though she did on a burglar one night! She was simply trying to halt them from touching her.

Eventually, after "Please don't touch my dog" and "If you touch her she will bite you" failed, I became aware that I needed another plan, fast. With each success she had at 'scaring away a threat' she got more confident, and progressively she was becoming actively aggressive, occasionally trying to chase people away before they looked like they might touch her.

So I developed a new saying that worked really well, and I offer it to anyone in a similar situation.

"She has *bad mange*. Don't touch!" The emphasis is on the words 'bad' and 'mange'. It's brilliant. Their hand recoils immediately and horror fills their face, and they often turn and go immediately. Sometimes running.

That stopped them.

And then came the crucial learning point, the thing I learnt that has helped other dogs time and time again. Slowly Lace began to realise that what I was saying to oncoming humans who wished to touch her was making them back off and go away. When she realised that I was resolving the problem without her having to take action, she relaxed a lot more around people and if a stranger approached she would look up at me to see if I was going to take action and say the magic 'mange' word. As I did so more and more, so she stopped reacting to and displaying at them.

Over several years she made many human friends, adults and children, but always at her pace and in her own way. I understood the crucial learning point here: that dogs like Lace were not nasty, but they had been increasingly pressured into protecting their personal body space, because their owners, including Lace's first owner and at the beginning me, had failed to support and protect them. I've seen dozens of dogs with this same problem and the solution always revolves around the owner finding a successful way of keeping strangers at bay and keeping their dog feeling safe and protected from people and their prying hands.

With dogs like Lace, management of the dog, training an instant recall, instant distance 'down' or 'sit' and a firm 'leave it' command for emergencies are essential if you have a people-biter. And these days, now that they are freely available, a muzzle is the safest option until full control is established, and probably beyond that.

When it comes to people-aggressive dogs of this type it's important to remember that the dog's faith in humans and a more relaxed attitude toward them can only be achieved once an effective method of keeping unwanted contact away can be found, and applied.

The dog must have faith that the owner is reading the dog's discomfort signals, and responding to them, before there is any chance that the dog will allow the owner to make the judgement for them. If the dog doesn't trust the owner, then it is likely to continue to defend its own body and personal space: it will probably keep biting people.

When a dog bites a person under these types of circumstance, it is very often simply a request for space. It wants the human, or that part of the human (often hands or arms), to go away. If after it bites the human, the human does 'go away', then the dog learns that biting humans is effective. *So it usually becomes more likely that it will bite in the future.* Sadly, what the dog doesn't learn or know is that it is potentially performing a highly illegal action when it removes a human in this way. And it's possible it might end up being destroyed for this action.

When it comes to dogs that bite humans, there are several different potential reasons; it isn't always about unwanted attention. From a trained police dog apprehending a criminal to someone touching a tired, sleepy dog, taking it by surprise, to a dog defending its territory, to a dog that is trying to resource-guard its space, owner, food, toy or bed; all of these issues can be improved by careful management. Most of them can be improved by great training, but it is essential that the underlying causes are resolved before anything is going to be truly successful.

Lace had done nothing wrong in my view. She went on to be not just a great agility and obedience dog, but also a wonderful companion to me, and a surrogate mum to Cloud. She protected both old Cassie and puppy Cloud from other dogs, and me once from a burglar. She also went on to be a great teaching dog for my agility students. I often handed her to a student so that they could see where their handling skills were going wrong. Lace was hugely trainable and highly obedient and responsive, and she helped many learn the art of agility as well as teaching me about people-biting, inter-dog aggression at home (she fought with Cassie), scentwork (she was an incredible search dog), and sound-based fears, anxiety-related conditions and many other things. As my friend, she was second to none and I felt privileged indeed to have spent so many years with this wonderful girl who loved me so. She was put to sleep at the grand old age of nineteen. I still miss her terribly.

Run free, little Lace, my wonderful friend. May your legacy live on…

Let sleeping dogs lie. And never touch a strange dog. For if you do, it might bite you and no one will feel sorry for you because it will be your own fault!

Tia: The Creation of a People-Biting Dog!

One of the great things about running dog-training classes is that each week, the dog you saw last week comes in again and sometimes there has been a dramatic change. The obvious thing with puppies is how much bigger they have grown. A week's growth in a young puppy can be jaw-dropping at times. But it is important to remember that it's not just the body of the dog that is growing and changing; it is also its mind, temperament and personality, its view of the world, its behaviour and its reactions to things.

We once had a dog in class that taught me a great lesson about how behaviours begin and develop. She was a lovely little pup when she came in, an English Bull Terrier cross called Tia. She was around ten weeks old and she was a normal puppy doing normal things, but she had a lovely lopsided, cute look to her. Her ears did funny things and she had a patch over one eye that gave her the comical look of a cartoon dog.

During classes, after explaining a process or technique that we are about to practise, it is common for me to ask to borrow a puppy or dog with which to demonstrate the technique so people can see it in action. I choose the candidate very carefully. To start with I make a kissy noise to get the puppies' or dogs' attention, then some will look at me and some won't. Some will wag their tails and pull forward on their leads, seemingly shouting, "Me, me, choose me!"

Others will stand their ground but watch me for the next few seconds. Others still will ignore the sound and carry on doing what they are doing. I choose one of the ones that appear to want to come to me.

And so it was with Tia. She looked up and pulled toward me and I leant over and took her lead. By this time she was around thirteen weeks old. She trotted beside me, looking up at me, knowing that I had liver cake and her owners just had chicken. She liked liver cake better. Although she had seemed keen to come to me, she didn't seem overly friendly. She didn't wag her tail or try to jump up me, or lick me, or wriggle into my hands or legs. Instead she just walked with me, wondering how soon the liver cake would come. That was fine by me. It's easier to demonstrate with a pup who just wants to learn to get the praise and food, rather than one that feels it wants to leap onto me, go all silly and wriggly and forget the learning process and instead dissolve into some giddy, frantic, madly happy thing, as some puppies do when I take their lead. She was an intelligent animal, I already knew, and she wanted to do whatever she needed to do to get the liver cake. She wasn't interested in being fussed or stroked, just food and learning. I respected her for that and I never tried to touch her or bend over her or stroke her. I smiled at her and praised her and offered her the food when she had done well, and we both got along just fine.

We walked into the centre of the room and did the demo, which she performed brilliantly, and then I returned her to her owners for them to have a go. She was nonplussed about being handed back and she paid no more attention to her owners than she had to me.

Through the time she spent in class I observed, as I had

many thousands of times before with other dogs, that Tia was not really that interested in people, even her owners. She liked dogs more, but she wasn't overly fussed with them either. She was a little aloof, even with her owners. She was interested in her environment, in food, and she liked to sit and watch things and sniff and suss things out. She was not a socially extroverted dog. Many aren't, and there is nothing wrong with that. I likened her to the contemplative child who sits at the back of the classroom taking everything in, but not really drawing attention to themselves. That quiet child could well be the one who, having spent more time thinking and observing than talking and socialising and 'fitting in', goes on to make a fantastic observation or discovery about the way the world works. I doubt Tia went on to resolve the mysteries of quantum mechanics or how to create perpetual motion, but she certainly in her own way made a big difference to the world.

I was not concerned about Tia. She was definitely at the aloof end of the spectrum, but she was still a normal, regular dog. About eight weeks into her training she was doing well, streaking ahead of the class in terms of learning and accomplishing tasks. Once again I needed to borrow a puppy and I made the kissy noise to see who was willing to help me out. Tia looked up at me in an interested way, but for the first time she didn't pull on her lead toward me. I was disappointed; she had fast become my favourite demo pup, and one of my favourite animals in the class. I admired her intelligence. So instead I chose the dog on her immediate right to help with the demo. As I moved toward the little Spaniel that was so keen to come to me, I passed in front of Tia, quite close, within maybe a foot or so, and as I did, I heard a low, rumbling growl that surprised me. Was that little Tia? I looked, and she had taken a step back away from me. I collected the Cocker, did the demo and set the class practising the exercise and then I went over to Tia's owners and asked if they had heard the growl. Yes, they had. It wasn't the first time she had growled, they told me. This week she had growled at three people including their eight-year-old daughter.

This change in Tia's behaviour concerned me greatly and I advised them that I considered Tia to be aloof and needing space and encouraged them to call me the next day to have a proper chat, but to ensure that they stopped people from stroking her or approaching with immediate effect, until after we had spoken. I advised them to respect her need for space, to let her sleep when she wanted to and to ensure that their children never touched her when she was resting or sleeping. The growl to the daughter had been a consequence of the daughter grabbing Tia when she was sleeping. She wasn't frightened of people, she just preferred watching them to being approached or touched by them. Whilst not perhaps what the family had hoped for in a dog, it was still normal behaviour for many. I told them of my experience with Lace and the success of the mange story in an effort to help them protect Tia from unwanted advances.

Sadly, they were disheartened that I had diagnosed their dog as 'aloof'. Their previous dog, a Labrador, had been super friendly and they had wanted another like it. So, not wanting to believe me, they decided instead to go onto an internet forum to seek further advice, hoping no doubt that I was wrong and there was some miracle cure for aloof, growly dogs. The people on the internet forum had little experience but a lot of enthusiasm, it seemed, and they had advised all sorts of things: using food to distract the dog when it growled, getting strangers to feed the dog, using a ball to make the dog happier around people, wearing a ThunderShirt (a tight jacket intended to make the dog feel secure) to stop her from being 'so frightened', taking the dog out and getting her more socialisation. So, having perceived socialisation to mean 'get lots of people to stroke your dog', they took Tia down to the school gates and as the children and parents filed past her, they asked people if they would stroke Tia. As the children and adults obliged in stroking her the owners had held her still and if she growled they told her off. They decided to do this every day until they returned to class. But on the second day things went badly wrong – Tia had lunged at a child as it approached, hand outstretched. They had admonished Tia and taken her home in disgrace.

The following week they arrived at class and I was unaware of what had happened at the school. But I was immediately aware that Tia's attitude was very different. She now sat motionless, watching as I greeted everyone from the middle of the room. As I made the kissy noise to find a puppy to demo with, Tia backed away and growled at me from over four metres away. I later asked the owners what had gone on, and with heads lowered in embarrassment, they told me about the school gates incidents. They knew they had made a mistake as they could see for themselves how much more aloof Tia had become, even with them.

As we talked, Tia sat away from all of us, looking at a dog on the other side of the room. Her body was positioned so that she was not facing us or away from us; she was sort of sideways on. It was clear that she was signalling her lack of desire to communicate with either me or her owners.

Imagine again that you are walking down the street holding hands with your young daughter and a strange man approaches and says, "Can I stroke your daughter?" Not wanting to offend the man, you agree. He looks a bit scary, best to not upset him. He strokes your daughter and she is clearly uncomfortable and looks to you for help. You see her discomfort but you stand your ground, holding her hand tightly so she cannot run away from the stranger and he can continue his stroking to his satisfaction.

How do you think this will have affected the relationship between you and your daughter? If I were your daughter I would be horrified that you didn't protect me from the strange man, that you observed my discomfort and yet did all you could to contain me so that I couldn't get away from it. I'm not sure that I would trust you again. Somewhere deep down I would acknowledge to myself that my parent allows bad things to happen to me and is not to be trusted. Without a parent (or owner) that you can trust, the world, which is confusing and weird at times for all of us, becomes a much more worrying place.

When a dog tries to avoid contact with another person, another dog, or indeed anything that it doesn't wish to have contact with, then one has to be very careful to respect that. It is not within the nature of all dogs to like everyone and everything, any more than it is in my nature to like cooking or cleaning or sewing, or other domestic, 'female' chores. I hate them. And now after the school gates incident, Tia was beginning to hate people.

Over the coming months I spent a lot of time with Tia's owners and we walked our dogs together. As we walked I explained the difference between their dog and my dogs. I pointed out where Tia was signalling for space and I showed them how they could protect her from oncoming hands by stepping in front of her and using the mange line, as well as a lead saying *Please don't touch*. As Tia began to realise that her owners were protecting her from oncoming strangers, she began to regain her trust in them and their decisions and the growling lessened. She also benefitted from spending time with my three older, wiser, worldlier dogs. She learnt to chill out a bit and one day, when she arrived at my door for her third walk, she wagged her tail at me. Not for long and not in a big way, but in a happy, pleased-to-see-me way. She had come to enjoy the company of another person and another three dogs, because we all did fun things together, but neither I nor my dogs bothered her in any way. If Tia wanted contact they would play with her, but if she didn't they would leave her alone and so did I.

Walking dogs that have challenges with other dogs that can comfort, protect, teach or lead them is a great way to change behaviour and I am quite sure that without intervention from me and my dogs after the school gate incident (or somebody else and their dogs, if not mine), Tia's fate would have been a little less happy. She was starting on a slippery slope towards causing real harm and losing either her home or her life.

By coming to understand Tia's view on life, the family realised that she wasn't really being a bad dog. Nor even, to be honest, was she really being that unfriendly. She wasn't attacking people randomly or chasing after them, she was just asking them to leave her alone. As it turned out, after a medical check-up Tia was diagnosed with some painful swelling of unknown origin around her spine and once the family realised that she was also in pain, they could see why she was so fed up with being touched when she was resting or bothered by strangers. We can all be tetchy if we wake up with pain in our backs or heads.

In fact pain is often involved where dogs are being grumpy, aloof, or showing aggressive signals. It should always be considered and proper, experienced veterinary help should be sought in cases where there is any likelihood of behaviour being pain-related. Most dogs and other animals have a tendency to carry a lot more pain within them before they show any obvious outward signs of it than humans do. Most people can spot that their dog has a problem if it becomes suddenly lame or shows obvious signs of discomfort, but many dogs will harbour quite large tumours, or serious skeletal, muscular or ligament and other pain without any obvious symptoms. *In fact sometimes the only symptom of pain can be aggressive signals, or not wanting to be bothered.* If your dog ever shows a sudden behavioural change that leans toward it being aggressive, or grumpy, or unusually aloof or distant, then a vet's opinion is a first port of call, before a trainer or behaviourist, I suggest. Unless it is known that the visit to the vet will compound the problem further (the dog is terrified of or aggressive with the vet), in which case I would look at behavioural first and veterinary after. In the past when I have noted behavioural changes in my dogs I have sought agreement from my vet to offer painkillers to my dog for a period of two weeks, to see if the behaviour resolves or changes. I prefer this route to a general anaesthetic for scans and X-rays. If after being on painkillers the dog's behaviour improves then that can definitely point toward a pain-related behaviour change.

Medication did a lot to resolve Tia's discomfort, and she was given both a brightly coloured lead and a fancy new jacket that had the words *Please don't touch me* written on it, which meant that people were much less likely to do so. Just like Lace before her had done, as Tia became aware that all of a sudden people had started to leave her alone, she relaxed a lot and she began to initiate more affection with her owners. At home she was given her own cage, a safe space, which was made very comfy inside and the children and family made a new rule that when Tia was in her cage or asleep or resting she was to be left very much alone. Tia was happier, the family was safer and the strangers were kept at bay.

The case of Tia was a long time ago. But to the best of my knowledge there were no further problems with her.

Understanding and clarity can often bring very dramatic results in terms of behaviour change. This family did nothing wrong; they just did what they thought was right. The problem occurs when the humans and the dogs disagree about what is and what isn't right. At classes we began to implement a very basic temperament test for dogs so that owners could see for themselves the difference between their dog's approach toward other dogs and humans, compared to the approach of the other dogs in the class. When you see a series of dogs approach a human or another dog you can see the differences in their attitude much more clearly than anyone can explain it. Some (typically Labradors) can have very over-the-top, even annoyingly over-the-top, friendly reactions, whereas other breeds, particularly the guarding breeds and some of the herding breeds, some terriers, and other breeds or individuals within breeds, can be much more aloof and owner-focused, or even insular and distant.

But what is clear from this is that if all humans adhered to the two rules – let sleeping dogs lie, and never touch a dog unless you know it *and* you know it is friendly and asking to be touched – then dogs like Lace and Tia would never have developed the issues they did in the first place. And there would be far fewer bite incidents in the world!

Belle: "A Right Little Bugger!"

The number of times I have received phone calls or emails telling me that an owner has an 'aggressive puppy' must be in the hundreds. Most often a new owner, perhaps unfamiliar with dogs, is worried when their puppy sometimes growls or snarls, or mouths vigorously and pulls at their hands or trousers. This can be enough to warrant a panic in some owners that the new love of their life, their cute, fluffy little puppy, is in fact a savage monster.

Part of this is simply inexperience, but I also believe that there is creeping intolerance of 'aggression' in dogs that has begun to pervade the human psyche, bringing about a belief that aggression in dogs is common, unacceptable, and that their dog is 'one of them'.

There are so many reports these days of 'dangerous dogs' and it can be all too easy to think that there are millions of them out there, when actually, truly aggressive dogs, and certainly truly aggressive puppies, are in fact very rare. They do exist; there appear to be a lot more of them than when I was younger, but thankfully in my experience it is still very rare, even for someone in my line of work, to encounter many at all. At least that is the case in the areas I have most frequently worked – it may be different elsewhere in the world.

When Belle first came into my life there was no mention of aggression. She was thirteen weeks old and had come into one of our normal puppy classes, with no concerns noted on the registration form. Her owners were just short of retirement age, a lovely, worldly, confident couple who had owned dogs and horses all of their lives, were country people and very experienced dog owners and trainers. All of the puppies in the group were under five months and Belle was one of the youngest, and certainly the smallest. During the class I noted that Belle was a little aloof with the other puppies and there was no wagging of tails or wriggly silliness that often accompanies a puppy's first session in class. She appeared fearless in this new and unusual environment, but other than that, she was responding well to the training and it was clear that of all the owners in the class, this couple had by far the most experience.

When I asked if anyone had any problems at home that they needed to talk about, Belle's owners said that they had brought this pup to classes because she seemed to be a very strong little dog, and for the first time in their lives they felt that they needed help to train a dog. So I watched more carefully to see if I could spot problems and again I observed that Belle, though not evidently unfriendly, seemed to show little interest in the other puppies. Occasionally, you do get puppies that have no interest in other puppies, sometimes because they have another dog at home, and they can decide that they have a friend (or friends) at home and therefore are less interested in making friends at class. Others can be somewhat overwhelmed at their first class by all the new sizes, breeds, colours, smells and behaviours of the other puppies. Then there are those that are naturally aloof. Some puppies seem to pair up with humans and have little interest in other dogs and that is just how they are. This, I suspected, or hoped, was the case with Belle.

The class was nearing the end and I had observed no puppies that were too frightened or overwhelmed to take part in off-lead socialisation, so I prepared the owners to let their dogs off lead to play. We asked the owners to spread themselves about the room and then, on my signal, to remove their leads. We released the dogs and the owners were asked to move around to keep the puppies from piling up in one place and overwhelming any individual pup. Everything was normal.

All of the puppies were released and unusually, Belle stayed focused on her owners, not seeming to realise that she was off lead. Some of the puppies immediately piled in to play and others tried to join in, but one pup, a Retriever slightly larger than Belle, ran over to her and placed a friendly paw on her shoulder, requesting play. The response from Belle was immediate, highly unusual and very dramatic. Belle whirled round on the larger puppy and with a skill that belied her age she rose on her hind legs, came down on the back of the bigger, older, Retriever, stamped on him and sank her puppy teeth hard into the neck of the bigger dog and began to shake it frantically and violently. Despite her lesser size the vigour of the shake lifted the older puppy off his feet and he issued that awful scream that puppies use to halt another dog's attack. Such a surprising amount of force and strength for such a small animal – Belle's reaction caught everyone by surprise.

As all heads turned towards the terrible sound of the screaming I ran across the short distance to the two puppies and grabbing Belle by her collar, pulled her off the terrified Retriever. She whirled round on me and sank her teeth into my hand and again began to shake. I had never been intentionally bitten by a puppy so young, and surprised, I did what I could to free myself from her shaking grip. As she released my hand she lunged at my torso, teeth bared, but I saw it and she was too small to reach her target so I was able to dodge the impact. Her owners stood back and watched with a wry smile on their faces and said, "There ya go, we told you she was a little bugger!"

A little bugger indeed!

As I talked to the owners of the Retriever, assuring them that their dog would be fine and if they looked they could see him already engaging with other puppies, I wondered how on earth such a young dog as Belle had come to be this way. I asked Belle's owners to stay behind and we chatted about her background.

They had only owned her a few days. In that short time they had realised that she was "a very determined dog", much more so than they had ever encountered before, hence why they had decided to come to classes rather than train her at home. They explained that she had also bitten the female owner as she had tried to get her into her cage one night, and that she had showed this extreme shaking behaviour with all of her toys at home.

I enquired about her breeding and the circumstances from which she had come. Belle had been bred by a terrier breeder who worked full-time in vermin disposal. His dogs ran as a pack and were used to clear farmyards and other places of mice and rats. The puppies had been running loose with the older dogs as it had been the breeder's habit to 'teach them the trade'.

I had seen working packs of terriers in action as a child. I had watched with fascination and some horror as I'd seen the swift effectiveness with which a pack of terriers could hunt down, catch and despatch dozens of rodents with brutal, lightning effectiveness in the space of a few minutes, and I thanked the universe that the puppy who had tried to play with Belle that day had been so much bigger than her!

I explained to the owners that Belle had, in my view, both a genetic predisposition and some learned behaviour in place that made her worryingly likely to behave this way towards other dogs and potentially other animals, and that unlike most puppies, I didn't recommend that she be let off the lead with young or small dogs again until we could figure out a way to make her safer to be around.

"So what could we do to help?" they enquired.

I offered the chance to run her with my dogs. I was sure that although she was certainly fierce towards the other pup that day, she was likely to be more respectful towards much older, bigger dogs. I figured she would no doubt have learned how to show respect to older dogs from the pack in which she had been running before she was sold to her new owners. And I also knew that my dogs, highly socialised and practised at diffusing a variety of challenging situations, would most likely be able to read and manage this young hooligan. Less than a foot tall and with only puppy teeth, I knew that Belle wouldn't be able to cause any injury to them as she would barely have the strength to bite through the thick neck ruffs of my long-coated dogs, let alone cause damage with her tiny teeth, and she certainly wouldn't outmanoeuvre dogs as wily and experienced as mine.

I explained to the owners what I planned and also that my dogs were quite likely to get cross if Belle was rude, that they might shout and knock the pup over or push her roughly away, but that they were used to dealing with such things and would have no intention of causing damage. As very experienced owners they were happy to let Belle have a rollocking if necessary; they knew dogs need to learn and they were just grateful that we were still willing to help them, as they were already aware that this little dog was more of a handful than anything they had encountered before. Indeed, this little dog was more of a handful than anything *I* had encountered before as well; at least for a dog of this age.

At that time I had Cloud, Connor and Mirk, and we routinely ran them with pups and other dogs so that less experienced animals could learn manners and respectful behaviour. Letting pups run with adults also gives pups that have no other dog at home to learn from the chance to mimic sensible adult dog behaviour. These adult/pup lessons are so crucial for successful development for so many youngsters in that situation, and we were lucky at that time to have a whole group of dogs to choose from that frequently ran together with the specific intention of teaching less experienced dogs.

Each of my dogs had characteristics that would help Belle learn and hopefully become a more informed and amenable character.

So we brought in Connor. Connor was young but highly social, gentler than Cloud and more alert and able to read signals than old Mirk was. He wasn't keen on puppies, but at that time he would tolerate them unless they were rude.

We brought Connor in and he eyed the pup suspiciously. It was clear from Belle's reaction that she was interested in Connor, where she had not been interested in the pups in class. Her little stumpy tail stood tall and stiff and she stood erect and alert and eyed Connor back. Connor quickly lost interest in her, and off lead he trotted round the room confidently, looking for a ball or toy to take to someone to be thrown. Confident that Connor had had time to read the pup and happy that he was unconcerned but interested, we let Belle's lead drop so that she could drag it around, but effectively be free. The lead was there to remove her quickly if we needed to. She ran assertively towards Connor and as she drew alongside Connor's moving body she leapt up to grab rudely at his ruff. Connor had read the approach correctly and he twisted his head around, opened his mouth and roared at the youngster, reminding her to be respectful. Belle looked mildly shocked and fell to the floor, halting her leap. She then stood and with head and tail lowered slightly, she curled her back in a polite gesture to Connor. Connor, having no interest in the pup, seemed to ignore the apology and losing interest, he immediately wandered off again. No sooner did Connor start to move than the pup recovered her confidence and again ran to Connor, who was strolling away, and jumped at his neck again. Connor, never liking puppies but controlled in his response and cool as a cucumber, intercepted her lunge, opened his mouth and allowed the little pup's head to enter it completely, effectively catching her like a ball. With an almighty roar and a flick of his head, he tossed the youngster, by her head, but in a measured way and without causing injury, to one side.

The pup recovered quickly but recognised she was outsized and outclassed. She lowered her stiff little tail, curled her back and rolled over briefly, showing Connor her belly. Connor glanced at her tummy and then wandered off as if uninterested, and Belle just stood and watched him go. This pup was more confident and bold than anything I had ever encountered to that day (though not since), and she was going to be a handful, of that I was quite sure! The interaction had gone well. The pup had learned that not all dogs will tolerate rudeness and that Connor was able to toss her away.

The following week we went through the same process with Connor and Belle was more respectful, so we brought in old Mirk. Mirk, despite his age, was exceptionally sociable and liked puppies. So we let her in and Mirk, tail wagging and genuinely friendly, stopped to sniff the pup. Belle at first was very respectful to the twelve-year-old, big, entire male dog. It was fascinating to me that this little, now fourteen-week-old pup knew so many appeasement signals. She curled away from Mirk and stilled as Mirk sniffed her, showing experience beyond her few weeks. She issued all sorts of appeasement to Mirk and for a few moments Mirk, always up for being friends with puppies, wagged his tail and lowered his head politely and in friendship. But with the initial polite greeting over, Belle quickly grew in confidence and began to leap and bound around Mirk's face, yapping, so Mirk feigned a lack of interest and wandered off. Belle pursued him and, barking, tried to grab at Mirk's incredibly thick ruff. Mirk just carried on walking, showing no response at all, as if the pup wasn't there. Feigning a lack of interest is a great teaching skill and can work wonders for very reactive dogs, but this little dog would not stop and she kept leaping with increasing aggression and rudeness as Mirk wandered over to me to check for food in my pockets. All the way, Belle leapt and bounded at Mirk's neck until suddenly, Mirk, as Connor had before him, turned his head and with a surprising loudness that shocked even me, roared at the little pup. Belle was caught off guard and stopped briefly. But within seconds she had recovered and leapt once more at Mirk's neck. Mirk remained unconcerned, but it was clear that Belle was growing in confidence and Mirk was probably not strong enough a dog to stop it, so I decided that as Belle was getting more pushy, not less, we needed to bring in the big guns, to really teach her that some dogs are not to be messed with.

So we went to get Cloud.

Cloud had by this time become the dog that took charge of all doggy situations. She had been pivotal in the resolution of many dozens of dog reactivity and aggression cases. She had an amazing talent to give confidence to frightened dogs, but to really knock the wind out of the sails of overly pushy, or aggressive dogs. I think it was best to say that she didn't suffer fools gladly. For years Cloud had almost single-handedly ceased reactivity in so many dogs; she could split fights between much bigger dogs with ease. Very few dogs ever messed with her despite the fact that most often, she just ignored them and had no real contact, unless she either fancied them, or they needed her help in some way, or they were rude and disrespectful to her. She would without fail stop any dog from fighting, causing a fight, staring, jumping up at people, barking unnecessarily, or jumping up worktops. Indeed anything she was told not to do herself, she would stop other dogs from doing. Cloud was amazing.

We had grown confident in allowing Cloud to assess a dog for us, relying on her response to any particular dog to tell us whether a dog that was in for aggression assessment was aggressive, frightened, just all mouth, or something else. She had a talent that was evident to everyone who met her and we knew that she would suss out this dog and act accordingly. Some of the things she just 'did' without training seemed almost miraculous. She did things that none of us could have done, with ease.

She came into the room and Belle stood tall and still. There was a slight glimmer of doubt in her eyes as Cloud looked back at her with her piercing amber eyes that unnerved so many as they seemed to bore right into the soul, but Belle just stood there anyway. Cloud looked Belle's way for a few seconds and then, with what looked like a 'dirty look' at her, she trotted off. Belle charged after her but before she could even leap at Cloud's neck, Cloud whirled round on her, opened her mouth and roared. Belle stopped in her tracks and backed off one pace; Cloud advanced, roared again; Belle backed off further. Cloud roared again and then stared at Belle for a few seconds, whereupon Belle turned and fled. Cloud moved off, unconcerned, and feigned a lack of interest but I could see that she was watching Belle as she moved away. Belle eyed her from the other side of the room, and now showing signs of respect she slowly tried to advance on her again. It was clear that Cloud did not like this at all and she wouldn't tolerate her presence from closer than a few metres. Every time Belle advanced Cloud stared at her, halting her advance, or if it didn't halt her advance she chased her and roared at her. I had never seen a dog try so many times to advance on Cloud. Normally after one stare or roar from Cloud they backed off permanently but this little pup was determined to get closer. Despite the fact Belle was clearly just a puppy, Cloud didn't cut her any slack at all. She meant business.

And so it proceeded. Each day after class we would mix Belle with my dogs and she would slowly learn that she couldn't get away with much with them, and she became more and more respectful. If she was in a particularly stroppy mood we would put all three of my dogs with her. But still I advised that I considered her unfit to mix with smaller, younger or weaker dogs than her, and that she should be muzzled for safety in the presence of other dogs. Her owners seemed resigned to and accepting of this. They had had a few bad experiences with her out on walks and they didn't want anyone's dog to get hurt. After eighteen weeks of training, when she became by far the best dog in class in terms of obedience, they left to lead their lives together.

Eighteen months later I had a call from them to say that they were reaching the end of their tether with this dog, that she had bitten both of them several times, and that she guarded her cage and the dining room table. Additionally, she had recently begun "attacking water" with such violence that they had been unable to intervene for fear of being bitten. They were now very frightened of her and were no longer enjoying walking or living with her. Attacking water was not something I had heard of and I was curious to understand and keen to help, so we arranged for a private lesson at their home.

On my arrival, Belle was stood on top of the beautiful antique dining room table and she regarded me as she might a displeasing view. She glared at the owners too, daring us to advance. I chose not to. They described how they had found a place to walk where there were few dogs, but that over time she had come to ignore all other dogs anyway and was only a problem if they approached her, when she would attack violently. They could no longer get the muzzle on her so they warned other owners to keep their dogs away. They had been taking her to places where she could swim, to tire her, but one day she had begun to attack the water with such violence and intensity that they had been unable to interrupt her or call her out of the water. On her last visit to the lake she had stood in the water and had aggressively tried to grab the water droplets that she herself had made by thrashing about. When the husband, unable to recall her out of the water, had decided after two hours to wade in to get her, Belle had turned her attack on him and had bitten straight through his wellies.

The reason for the call, however, was that yesterday, for the first time, Belle had attacked a puddle in the street with as much force as she had the lake, so now even walks around her home were becoming depressingly worrying experiences. I wanted to see this in action so we planned a trip to the shallow lake that Belle so loved.

The owner put Belle on her lead and let her out onto the driveway, confident that she would immediately run to the car, dragging her lead behind. She stood happily wagging her tail, looking from the husband to the car door handle, wanting for it to open. Then she jumped in joyfully straight into her cage, and sat waiting for the journey to begin. We all piled into the car. I sat in the back seat with Belle beside me in her small cage. She regarded me silently from her position. It was not a look of friendliness. I noticed that I was growing increasingly uncomfortable with her stare. She had seen a vet and despite brain scans and many tests the vet had found nothing medically wrong. Her food was good and her exercise was also most adequate. So other than her breeding and whatever lessons her eighteen months of age had provided her, I couldn't understand her apparent distaste for me. But at that moment I felt she would have gleefully killed me if she could.

We arrived at the field with the lake in it and pulled into a dead end road, full of neat little semis, to park and walk onto the field. Once in the field, the owners released Belle from her lead and she ran excitedly off towards the lake, trailing the long line I had requested so that we could keep control no matter what happened. Immediately she entered the water and began her ritual of attacking it. I'd never seen a dog do anything like this before, as she raged and roared and grabbed at the water droplets and shook her head as if killing each drop. She was like a wild demon as she roared and pounced and grabbed and shook. The whites of her eyes grew increasingly visible and her whole torso was tense with energy and intent.

Very quickly I'd seen enough and wanted her out, so I threw in a floating retrieve toy on a rope and tried to gain her attention with it to get her away from the lake. As I repeatedly threw the toy near her, she saw it but instead of grabbing it as I'd hoped, she just tore with increasing vigour at the water. Finally after several minutes and several throws she appeared to lose her temper with the toy and pounced on it, grabbing it and shaking it so forcefully that I felt surprised her head didn't shake off. I pulled her in as she clung, shook, tore and snarled at the toy.

Well at least I had had success with the retrieve toy, and I explained to her owners that this was something we could build on. We set off back across the field to return to their house to chat and come up with a plan. I was beginning to think that with time and effort the retrieve toy might help them to extract her from the lake and I was starting to feel as if, despite my initial reservations, I had got some answers I could share with them.

As we walked together through the little housing estate, there came another surprise for me.

"How will we get her back in the car now, then?" they enquired of me.

"What do you mean?" I responded.

"Well, the last time we came here we couldn't get her back in the car. Just around the corner from here she started to go wild and attacked us and wouldn't let us take her near the car! It was terrifying. We haven't been here since. Sorry, perhaps we should have told you before?"

Inwardly my eyes rolled sky high as I repeated their words in my mind. *Perhaps we should have told you before?* I echoed to myself.

"Well, how did you get her home then… Last time?"

"My husband had to walk her," the wife said, looking worried again.

Realising that we had been in the car for some time to get there, I enquired, "You walked her? How far is it?"

"Oh, it's nearly three hours."

Three hours? I had to start classes in less than three hours! My heart sank.

Perhaps they should have told me. Or perhaps I should have asked!

Lesson learned. If ever you are going in a car with a case dog, make sure to ask if she'll get back in the car easily enough on the way back. Since this case I have met other dogs who will not get in or out of the car because it's not what they want to do. In fact, don't go in the car with a case dog; go in your own car, and follow their car.

No sooner were the words out of his mouth than we

rounded the corner to where we could see the car. Belle had been ahead of us all, pulling determinedly on her lead, but as soon as she saw the car she stopped and started to growl, first at the car and then she turned her attention to the husband, who held her lead. Her hackles raised and her lips curled and her body went rigid as she stared at the owner. And then after a second or two she swung back her head and grabbed the lead, shaking it violently, growling and snarling as if in the killing frenzy of a hundred dogs.

"Here, you have her," said the man, hurriedly passing the lead to me. As he released the lead, Belle let the lead go too and lunged for him, mouth open, and grabbed at his trouser belt, shaking briefly and letting go. Surprised, I took the lead and no sooner had I done so than Belle stopped her attack on the man and instead turned her attention to me. She froze and glowered at me.

I froze too and looked back at Belle and then after just a few seconds, she again launched herself at the lead, and shook it even harder than she had before.

A Jack Russell in a shaking frenzy is a very worrying thing to see, and it can be noisy, too.

By this time the noise of Belle's growling and snarling had drawn the attention of two small groups of people close by. Over the top of Belle's head I could see some mildly amused, others looking rather concerned, frightened even, onlookers watching with interest as the situation played itself out.

At the same time as I saw them, I realised two things at once.

Firstly, at that precise moment I couldn't begin to imagine how this situation might end, or indeed how we might get Belle back in the car.

And secondly, because I was set to go to classes after this appointment, I was wearing my sky blue jumper with the

CaDeLac logo emblazoned upon it, advertising who I was and what I did for a living.

CaDeLac Dog Training and Behaviour, my back announced proudly.

If I was to fail here, with this dog, I was to fail very publicly and possibly very painfully.

Oh pooh! I thought.

Needing time to think, I took a step back away from the wildly snarling and shaking Belle and the car which she so wished to avoid, and turned the other way, heading back to the park. Belle responded immediately, as I hoped she would. She dropped the lead and strode forward in front of me, and with a keen tug she happily began to pull me back towards the park. After a few metres I halted her, and I entered a phase of what I call speed thinking.

Now it is important to remember that to succeed in any dog behaviour rehab process it is essential that the owners believe in you. No matter how good you might or might not be, if an owner does not have faith in you or believe in you then they are unlikely to follow whatever advice you can give. Even if it is great advice, if it requires effort on their part, which it almost inevitably does, then you need to get them to buy in to it. Because if they believe in you they will give it more time, more effort. In other words, no matter what happens, you have to stay cool. Even if you wish you could just disappear into a hole, you still have to stay calm, in order to have the best chance of helping the dog or owner.

Stay cool, on the outside. Shit yourself only on the inside.

I figured that if I tried to move Belle towards the car, she would react again and someone might get bitten again. So I decided to not even attempt that. Attracting Belle's attention with my hand, I tossed a few pieces of liver cake on the floor in the direction of the car to see what she thought of that manoeuvre. She wasn't impressed. She looked at the food, and the car behind it, and stayed where she was. *I am not going to fall for that trick*, her eyes told me.

I considered bringing the car closer so that we would have less distance to manoeuvre her but I felt the closeness of the car would still trigger a reaction and it wasn't worth the risk.

So, leaving Belle with her female owner where they were, the husband and I returned to the car to untie the rope keepers that were holding the dog's car cage in place on the back seat. If you can't get Mohammed to the mountain, bring the mountain to Mohammed. I would take the cage to her!

As we walked towards the car I could see that the crowd of onlookers was rapidly growing as mothers taking their children home from school had started to gather. There were parents with prams and children now standing watching us in fascination, as we freed the cage and carried it back across the road.

Belle, too, was looking on with interest. She appeared to have forgotten her desire to go back to the park for a moment and was watching us with a quizzical look on her face.

We walked past Belle with the cage, so that when we placed it on the ground she was looking in the direction of the park, not the car, as she looked into the cage.

I knew from earlier talks that Belle was trained to go into her cage for food, so I figured we would see if she felt the same way about the cage when it was placed in the street.

From experience of dealing with frightened and injured animals, I know that if you want them to do something they don't want to do, like walk through a gate, or into a stable or horsebox, then your best bet is to make the first attempt a success. Every failed attempt makes an animal more panicky, worried or angry and prepares them to take more evasive or dangerous action the next time. We had already failed to get her to approach the car once so I wanted this to work.

With that end in mind we secured the long line to Belle's collar. I then took the other end of the line and ran it through the open door of the cage and through the bars at the back, and from that position I held it, taking care not to tighten it, but having my arms and hands prepared to take the strain should I need to, should Belle not be willing to go into the cage. The cage was only two feet away from Belle, and she was still looking with curiosity. *So far, so good*, I thought. She hadn't made the connection that if we got her in the cage we could potentially get her in the car. As the female owner stood holding Belle, I instructed the husband to stand in front of Belle between her and the cage and with a handful of food to lower his hand to Belle's nose, allowing her to take a small piece from his hand, before tossing the rest of the treats into the cage for Belle to go in after, just as if he were sending her into her cage before bedtime at home.

Belle was still watching all the activity with interest. The owner stepped towards Belle and offered her the food. Belle, calm now, took the food and the owner tossed the rest of the food into the cage. Belle trotted in without issue and seeming relaxed, then reached down for a treat. No sooner had she taken the treat than her behaviour changed suddenly, as she whirled around and tried to make a fast escape from the cage, leaving the rest of the treats untouched. She must have realised that this was a set-up and she tried to make a fast exit. But this time I was ready for her and I pulled the long line tight, dragging her to the back of the cage. She snarled and screamed in protest and in an apparent rage, but she was stuck there. I yelled at the husband to close the door and I held on to Belle whilst the latches were closed. Then when she was safely confined I dropped the long line and felt the warm rush of relief.

As soon as the cage door banged shut, a big round of applause erupted from the onlookers and I suddenly remembered they were there. I felt myself blush, feeling half triumphant and half foolish for having got in this situation in the first place. But I also had a feeling of great sadness as I looked at Belle, and not for the first time, wondered what on earth would ever finally become of this little dog and the relationship with her worried and now frightened owners.

I looked at her owners and they both looked surprised and relieved. But there remained concern in their eyes as they looked at Belle, now safely in her cage.

We carried the cage gently back towards the car with an accompaniment of snarls and growls as Belle tried to bite us through the bars. As we lifted the cage into the car the onlookers began to lose interest and drift away. Belle glowered at me, even more than on the outward journey, but I got in beside her anyway for the journey home.

We sat and talked of all that had happened and I gave them some tips about teaching her how to latch on to a tug toy on a rope and use that to remove her from water if ever they needed to, without getting bitten. I also gave them some other tips about preventing her from guarding the table by restricting access to it, and some other bits and bobs.

But I did have to talk quietly and seriously about how I was overall quite concerned about her general behaviour and the risks that they were taking, living with her every day. They knew the problems that existed and they had seen for themselves today how she could easily have bitten me. I think they were already halfway to reaching the conclusion that Belle was not the dog for them, even before they had called me in. We chatted about the possibility of the breeder having her back where she might live a life that suited her temperament more. They said they would ask the breeder and try the things I'd suggested and get back to me in two weeks, unless they needed me urgently.

Belle's story, very sadly, does not have a happy ending and a few days later, I heard that following another serious and painful attack on the dog's female owner in the home, they had decided to have Belle put to sleep.

For a long time afterwards I worried that I did something wrong, that I should have done things differently, that maybe in some way I was at fault. But at the end of the day, I had to consider that this dog's genetics and background had made her a less than suitable candidate for a pet home.

When it comes to genetics in dogs it is important to remember that the main difference between Belle and the average black Lab, who wags their tail at everything that moves and never presents any aggressive behaviours through their whole life, is genetics; not environment, owner or trainer input.

The power of genetics in a dog should never be underestimated. If a dog or its predecessors have been bred specifically to perform an activity, be it hunting, herding, chasing, guarding, catching, killing or shaking, then there is a good chance that given an opportunity, these behaviours may well appear, whether they are appropriate to the home situation or not.

Guarding breeds have a tendency to show guarding behaviours.

Herding breeds have a tendency to show herding behaviours.

Hunting breeds have a tendency to show hunting behaviours.

And killing breeds have a tendency to show killing behaviours.

Especially if they have already seen those behaviours performed by others or if they have had a chance, or still have a chance, to practise them.

Not all animals within a breed will show these traits, but many will. There is a much better chance of getting a herding breed to herd than a game-flushing breed to herd. There is very little chance of getting a guarding breed to point, or a pointing breed to guard.

Generally speaking, in my experience, most dog owners choose their dog on what it looks like, not on what it was bred to do. In this case the owners were unlucky; they had had Jack Russells before that had not shown this behaviour.

Unfortunately, however, a dog's behaviour is determined more by what it is bred to *do* than what it looks like.

Looks *and* breed behaviours need to be considered when matching a dog in a forever home.

I have seen several Jack Russells with a very high prey drive, and a tendency to become snarly and snappy if they suffer frustration or don't have an outlet for their instincts. But I have also seen a fair few that are not like this, that do not possess their typical breed instincts. Whilst the breed does take up a lot of pages in my casebooks, I have known several who are truly delightful animals. Intelligent creatures; I've had several in my top obedience class and I have a friend whose Jack Russell is quite the sweetest little dog I have ever met!

Belle was not necessarily a 'bad' dog, though she might have been; rather she had been bred, very specifically and successfully, for killing vermin. Her parents had been good at their job and at an early age she had witnessed, and possibly been involved in, the act of killing vermin. It was the behaviour that she was bred for that had caused her downfall as a pet, not because she was necessarily a bad dog, but because she was in the wrong home. She would have been much more suited to staying in a ratting pack than walking around city parks.

Now the reasons for her finding herself in the wrong home, well, that is another story in itself!

Run free, little Belle.

Lad: A Child-Biter

This is a case from several years ago. A case that just goes to show that, until you see an animal in its home, you never can be sure of what's going on there. The story of Lad.

When the phone call came in I was advised that Lad, a year-old Border Collie, had begun to attack the owner's eight-year-old daughter. Apparently when the girl tried to move the dog leapt about her and if she tried to turn the lights on, in particular, the dog would jump up and bite. Bite incidents involving children are of course a pretty serious thing to face, and it was with some trepidation that I set off to see this case in his home. As well as the attacks I was told he was not house-trained and was manic, destructive and uncontrollable. Whenever I'm on my way to a case, my mind mulls over what information I have and I start to come up with ideas, plans, and I recall past cases. In this case I had plenty of time to think as I had a three-hour journey ahead of me. But it's not until I am there that things start to become clearer…

When I arrived I could see for myself that, yes, the dog was extremely hyper. On the way I had assumed that perhaps this young BC was under-stimulated. But the owner had had several Collies and seemed an avid dog fan. There was no doubt that this dog was loved. He was fed on steak and chicken and not much else, so we had to look at addressing the potential imbalance in his diet as a starting point. As we went through the dog's history I discovered that he was having five walks a day. His day started at 5.30am when the owner's partner left for work, walking the dog before he went. He then had four or more walks throughout the day.

As I took case notes I noted that the dog was continually pacing hither and thither, with frequent, rather random jumps onto the sofa, the owner, me and the child. The child in question was on the sofa with us, watching TV, but true to the reports, when she got up to move, the dog immediately leapt about her trying to nip at her arms, her hands and upper torso. Scratches and minor scrapes were already evident on the girl, who appeared not to be frightened of the dog; instead she just seemed resigned to her fate. So the dog was walked, but he never toileted outdoors and instead came in from his walk and toileted indoors. He had destroyed two sofas in his short life, and a double mattress. There were toys everywhere and he tossed them around and pounced on them throughout the time I was there.

Collies are my breed of choice, and I've met a lot of them. And I've met a lot of hyper ones too. In some cases under-stimulation or lack of exercise were partially to blame, but here, there was masses of stimulation and plenty of opportunities to walk. The dog also knew several of his toys by name and would, if requested, fetch a named toy, though when he brought it he would shake it madly, growling, and refuse to give it. We had a look at the dog's genetics: he was pedigree and I knew some of the lines, but I didn't see any real problems there. There are certain genetic traits in Collies – amber eyes, short coats, pricked ears, the red, blue or merle genes – all of which have certain character traits attached to them which can make them genetically more intense, nervous, flighty or just plain nutty. And yes, he had some of those genes floating about so there was a higher likelihood of genetic complexity, but still nothing truly explained the erratic and hectic behaviour of this dog.

My line of questioning was getting me nowhere in terms of understanding the cause of this dog's mania, and as I was floundering, the little girl stood up and offered to demonstrate what happened if she went near the light switch. The dog responded immediately, placing himself between the light switch and the girl. He leapt up, nipping at the girl's clothes as she lifted her arms out of the way and screamed at the dog. The dog leapt some more. I asked the helpful girl to sit down; I'd seen enough and wondered where this was leading, but she was determined to show me.

As she leant over the dog to switch on the light the dog launched at her, teeth bared, and grabbed her upper arm. Firmly but gently. The girl stopped briefly and then with the other arm swung over the dog's head and hit the light switch, illuminating the room. I hadn't noticed before but there had been windows open at the front and back of the house, creating a gentle breeze. There were wind chimes hanging here and there, tinkling metal ones and wooden clunky ones. Lovely sound, but as I looked up at the now-illuminated light above I saw the chandelier that was casting a shower of sparkling lights all around the room. The tinkling I'd heard was partially due to the sound of the chandelier.

The penny began to drop as the dog's franticness escalated and he began to charge around the room, woofing and pouncing on the shining reflections from the chandelier. It was almost like someone had charged up his batteries and he was now flat-out in manic activity. I turned the light off. The dog didn't react to me at all. Apparently, I then discovered, he never minded when anyone wanted to switch the light off, only when they switched it on. So, the dog was super-sensitive to the light and sound of the lighting fitment and possibly the wind chimes – but why? Was he ill? He looked well, but when

I looked closer I saw that there were slight swellings under his eyes. He looked like I looked in the mirror after a late night out or a challenging time in my life where sleep had been scarce. I'd never seen bags under the eyes of a dog before, so didn't know what it all meant. By this time I was somewhat mystified and although I had a few things in mind I still wasn't sure of the cause.

I'd discovered that although this was an experienced dog owner, pretty much all of her dogs had been rather manic, destructive and generally 'odd'. I wondered about toxic leaks near to the house, or something in the water perhaps, that could have affected several generations of unrelated dogs. Straws, clutch, at. So I delved further into his lifestyle.

"When the dog sleeps," I probed, "does he sleep on his side or in a sitting up or 'working' down position? And where does he sleep?"

And herein lay the answer. In one of the most surprising answers I'd ever heard from an owner: "Oh, I don't know, I've never seen him sleep."

Further delving led to the conclusion that in an effort to tire her dogs out to cease the madness she had come to know as 'Collies are like that', she had increased the stimulation and the levels of exercise, exacerbating what was an overly tired dog. The swellings I'd seen under his eyes were actually bags from sleeplessness. Until that day I didn't even consider that dogs got bags under their eyes from lack of sleep, but now I do. Dogs, like children and adults, can get increasingly tetchy and grumpy and manic as they become overtired and this young dog had never slept in front of his owner since she had brought him home as an older puppy. He had always been overtired! *Wow.* In addition, because of the overtired state of his mind, the dog simply couldn't cope with any more stimulation. The glittering, moving light patterns made by the light were too much for the dog to cope with. He had realised this himself, it seemed, for by jumping up and grabbing, but not hurting the humans, he was trying to stop them from turning on the source of his further excessive stimulation: the light. What he was saying was that he wanted to live without any more things to respond to. He wanted to be calmer. Surprisingly, most dogs do! They like being calm, but sometimes they don't know how to do it. Or can't, because their instinct is telling them to chase things that move. And light from a chandelier moves.

I'd seen a cage in the kitchen and I realised I'd failed to ask how often it was used. Apparently he went in there when he occasionally had a bone, but he had never been shut in there. So I suggested we take him there now, cover the cage with a thick, darkening cover, and see what happened. He trotted into his cage happily enough, we shut the door, covered the cage and stepped back. We hear him circle and lie down with a thump. Then within seconds we heard him snoring.

I learnt a lot that day. I learnt that some owners think that a shredded bed, a shredded child, a shredded sofa and a destroyed house are all normal, acceptable things when you own a dog! They are not, I advised her. I also learned that dogs that are 'mad' can be lacking sleep as well as lacking stimulation. In these days of internet forums and inexperienced persons giving inexperienced advice to other inexperienced persons, that *over*stimulation and *over*activity can be nearly as common a problem as bored dogs. I so often see people doling out advice to *increase* activity and stimulation for destructive or hyper dogs, when in fact some dogs need more sleep, not less.

I'd lost track of the progress of the case as the owner had moved house and I didn't have her new number, so I was surprised many months later when out of the blue, she wrote a review for me. In that review I learned that not only had both the destructiveness and the attacking of the daughter ceased that day, but the toilet training had somehow resolved itself too. I'd been told that Lad had previously been 'manic' when taken for a walk, overreacting to the sounds and movement of cars and other pedestrians and too busy to toilet, so I'd encouraged her to start again with toilet training using the cage method. Once the cage routine had been established he was much calmer on walks, had somehow retrained himself to toilet outside and never toileted indoors again. So after one good long sleep that day he had somehow learned to toilet outside again. Dogs are utterly amazing.

Sadly I heard recently that Lad has died, of age-related disorders.

I hope he is sleeping peacefully, right now.

Run free, Lad. Thank you for the lesson. Your memory lives on, here, in this book. Always. Run free.

Rosie: Until Death Us Do Part

When the phone rang I was busy doing something and I answered it feeling irritated and flustered. It was Sunday morning and I had a day of chores to get through, and at only ten o'clock this was the third call I'd had. Normally Sundays are quiet but today, when I least needed interrupting, everyone, it seemed, had a dog problem.

I hammered my finger into the answer button and said in a huff, "Hello."

Her words came tumbling out in a desperate scramble. "My vet suggested I ring you. We have a new dog, a Retriever, Rosie. We went to get a puppy but the woman said she wanted rid of the mother and that we could have her for free. We felt so sorry for her. We brought her home but she hasn't moved since she's been here. She won't eat or go to the toilet outside. Our vet said to speak to you and that if anyone could help, it would be you." The anxiety in her voice was clear and I put aside my other tasks to focus on the conversation. This lady's voice was weak with emotion. She was clearly labouring to get the details out. The case sounded heartbreaking.

"Could you come out now, please?" she concluded.

Now? Sunday morning? I'd got so many things to do. But she sounded so distressed. I really didn't have the time to spare, but it did indeed look like this dog needed help right now.

"What do you mean, she hasn't moved?" I needed clarity on those words.

"She has just lay still the whole time, since she came in the house."

"And when was that? How long has she been lying still?"

"We brought her home on Friday afternoon."

Friday? She had lain still for over thirty-six hours. I needed to see this dog straight away.

So setting aside my day, I set off to see this dog who had been lying still for so long.

When I arrived the door was answered by the lady I'd spoken to, who stood there with a finger on her lips, requesting me to say nothing and be quiet. She beckoned for me to come in. The house was dark inside, with no lights on. I was ushered into a front room where together with the father and teenage daughter, I was beckoned to sit down. There was no dog in this room and I wondered where she was. In hushed tones, the story was told to me.

They had decided to get a Retriever puppy. They had found an advert for a litter about fifty miles away and they had driven over, having been advised that there were puppies still available.

On arrival they had started to realise that this was not a litter from a family pet, or a caring breeder. They were led to a low-roofed, ramshackle building, which they were told the puppies and mother were in.

As they entered they had been struck by the terrible smell and the fact that the room was completely dark with no windows. They had heard frantic scuffling sounds as they entered. A dim old light had been switched on and they could then see at the back of a filthy, stinking pen, three Retriever puppies, all with brown staining on their golden fur from the terrible mess they were living in. They were still with their mother and all four of them were cowering at the back. The 'breeder' had stepped into the pen and lifted the puppies up and passed them to the family. The puppies had smelt awful and had scrabbled to get away from their grip.

The family had enquired as to why the animals appeared so frightened, and were told, "Oh, they don't get out much, they will be fine when you get them home."

Whilst the father and daughter had wanted a puppy, the lady of the family had looked at the old-looking bitch and felt so sorry for her. What a life for a beautiful old dog.

Seeing her looking at the mother, the breeder had said that this was to be her last litter. She was now looking for a new home for the old dog. Would she like an older dog instead of a puppy? She was giving her away free.

They all had had reservations about taking any animal from such a place but they couldn't bear to leave them all there. After a discussion outside the smelly barn, the family had decided that the old bitch was the one that needed a new home most and so they decided to forgo their planned puppy in favour of saving this old, sad-looking dog. A very noble and kind choice.

The old dog had been terrified in the car and had scratched them all when they tried to get her in. But somehow they had managed to get her home, although she had been sick and screamed during the long journey. But their problems were only just beginning. There was a frantic struggle as they had had to drag the terrified dog, squealing and scratching, out of the car and toward the house. She had tried hard to stay in the car but brute force had got her out. Once out, though, she had panicked and pulling the lead from the father's hands, had fled down an alley at the side of the house that led to the rear garden and there she had dug in under a hedge. It had taken a long time to get her out from under there and eventually drag her into the house as the rain had begun to pour down and they couldn't leave her there overnight. By this time the dog was completely overwhelmed, as were the family. Poor Rosie, dragged over the threshold into the house, had fled in panic again, through a door into the back room, and once in there she had collapsed. Panting heavily and with wide, frightened eyes, she had shivered and shaken so badly that they had finally decided to call a vet. At first they thought her just frightened, that she needed to sleep. But there had been no change overnight, so they rang their vet and asked him to come immediately.

The vet had assessed the exhausted dog, who had remained motionless during the assessment. After some tests the vet had diagnosed general poor health, rotting teeth and a urinary tract infection. He had given her a shot of antibiotics and painkillers but had said that in his opinion she might never recover from the ordeal and that they should either take her back, or put her to sleep.

Distraught, they had not taken the advice kindly and had asked the vet to leave their home. They then rang another vet and again insisted he come straight away. This vet had pretty much agreed with the first but had suggested that they call me, to see if my behavioural experience could help poor Rosie in any way. They had waited until the following morning to call me and by this time Rosie had had no food, no water, though it had been placed close to her, and had not been to the toilet in over thirty-six hours.

And so the time had come to see Rosie. Quietly and without turning on the light, I tiptoed into the room at the back of the house where she was. The room was in semi-darkness. The thoughtful family had kept the curtain closed as advised by the vet, as Rosie, until now, had been living in semi-darkness her whole life.

The smell was obnoxious. She smelt like a sewer on a hot summer day mixed in with the smell of rotting flesh and rancid infection.

As I approached her, she didn't react at all. Her eyes were open, her tongue lolled from the side of her mouth where it lay, apparently stuck to the wooden floorboards. Some of her teeth were exposed where her tongue lolled and I could see they were black, broken and sitting in swollen, infected gums. The smell from her mouth was even worse than the smell of faeces and urine that wafted up from her stained, rancid coat. Her eyes were fixed, glassy and unfocused, and she looked like a dog who had left this place and was residing mentally elsewhere. My stomach churned at the shocking sight before me and I felt sick and faint all at once. I gently knelt down beside her, trying not to disturb her and at the same time trying not to be sick.

The family stood behind me, peering silently, expectantly, no doubt hoping I could help in some way.

I didn't touch Rosie but I talked in low, hushed tones. She didn't respond at all.

I could see that her breathing was shallow and that she was utterly unresponsive. I guessed her whole body had just been overloaded with the fear of the last few days and I grew enraged inside at the person who had done this to her. Who could keep a dog in such a way and then rehome her to a lovely family, only to cause them such suffering and heartache? Who could do this to any animal? To any person? Why did anyone think that this was OK?

I sat for a while next to Rosie without speaking further or moving, just to see if there were any changes. Periodically her breathing would halt, but her eyes remained the same, fixed and glassy, as if she were almost dead. The only times I had seen animals like this before was when they had struggled to give birth and had been utterly exhausted from labour or had produced rotting offspring and their bodies had been overwhelmed with infection.

It was truly awful to see an animal in such a shutdown state. She was thought to be eight years old and had been kept in the barn her whole life, producing puppies. I could not imagine that she would ever recover from that kind of background and I really couldn't think of anything else that could be done other than offer her a pain-free exit from this world.

After ten minutes of sitting with Rosie and having no response at all, I got up quietly and returned to the front room to talk with the family. As I left the room, I stopped at the doorway to take one long last look at Rosie, knowing I would probably never see this poor animal again.

In my role as dog trainer, and particularly with behaviour cases, it is often necessary to encourage, motivate, enthuse and invigorate owners to do the things that need to be done to get the results they wish to achieve. I most often point out the strengths, the positives, and speak in terms of hope and success. I feel it's a common misconception that dog trainers work with dogs. True, dog trainers and behaviourists do certainly need a great understanding of dogs, but most often my role is dealing with owners, not dogs. It is the owners who have to do most of the work, or need to change their behaviour first. My role is to get them to a) realise this, and b) do it. Sometimes it's easy. Sometimes it's not.

In most cases after reaching my conclusion about what must be done I enjoy the "Well, this is what I think" bit. Often I have good news – I can help. Sometimes I have an explanation that makes an owner's face light up with sudden clarity or understanding. Sometimes I work hard to beef up a person's self-belief, or highlight their or their dog's potential, or bring up a series of good points that we can all focus on, or an unusual but positive solution that everyone can reach for and achieve.

This time I simply couldn't think of anything good to say. I genuinely didn't think that the dog should be allowed to continue to suffer. Even if she recovered emotionally, which I very much doubted, she was rife with infection and quite possibly pain in her teeth and I thought it was most likely she would need major veterinary work to remove several of them. And even without the teeth problems, she just didn't look well. She didn't look like a dog who wanted to recover. Would it be fair to let her continue this life? Indeed, *would* she continue? I doubted it. To me, she looked like she had given up and was just in the drawn-out process of dying.

We sat at the table in silence. I looked down for a moment at the table, hoping I'd get some inspiration from it. But nothing was forthcoming.

I looked up and all eyes were on me. They leant towards me, as if being closer might make things better. I could see the pleading in the women's eyes and the father sat stony-faced, staring at me, as if willing me to bring forth a miracle.

"I am so sorry," I began. "I'm afraid that I am inclined to agree with the vet, that the best thing for Rosie—"

The teenage girl, tears in her eyes, shot me an accusing look and got up from the table, intent on exiting the room before I'd even finished the first sentence. I noted though that even in her pain and anger with me, she remembered to open the door very carefully and close it behind her equally quietly so that Rosie would not be disturbed. This poor family – my heart was breaking for them. Tears appeared in her mother's eyes too. I looked back at the table for respite. At least the table wasn't crying. Yet.

I looked up. How could I ease their pain? How could I find the right words? I took a little time and searched and searched my mind. I didn't want to say the wrong thing.

After a few moments I gave it my best shot, but managed to say exactly the wrong thing.

"In all my years of dogs and animals I have never seen a dog so shut down with fear as your poor girl. The fact that she won't eat or drink and that she hasn't even toileted are not good signs at all. I cannot commend you enough on trying to save her from such appalling conditions and bringing her home to love and help her. But I think that for Rosie the move has maybe just been too traumatic." What a really stupid thing for me to have said. I cringed inside at my dumb words.

"You mean it's our fault?" Anger flashed in the mother's eyes.

I longed for the earth to open up and swallow me up completely, that I might be free from this terrible situation. How could I right this situation?

"Noooooooo. Not at all. Anyone with a heart would have done what you've done. I would have done what you've done. But I think that really, given her poor health and the fact that she is so used to living alone in the dark, she really is unlikely to ever recover."

I tried to ease the guilt I had just unintentionally created.

"Actually, looking at her, I think she probably would have died very soon anyway if you had left her there." I couldn't possibly know if she might have died or not. "Given the conditions you have described." I had no idea what would have become of Rosie, but I'm guessing that as she was no longer useful as a brood bitch, her fate at the breeder's might have been as grim as it looked right now.

I spoke for as long as I could about how wonderful I thought their actions had been to save this poor girl. How brave they had been. How kind and loving. I also said that I felt that at least Rosie had had some days in the warmth of a loving home and even though it hadn't made her better, I hoped that she might somehow know that love had surrounded her in the last few days.

The family decided to give Rosie a little while longer to see if she might recover and I left them to consider things, saying I would call later that day. The family had had visions of taking this poor, lost, unloved animal and making her fit and healthy, bathing her and making her smell of their kindness and love and expensive shampoo. They had visions of taking her to training classes, out walking in the woods and playing ball in the garden. I had already seen in the back room an expensive comfy dog bed in a shiny new indoor crate full of toys and teddy bears. They had prepared well to bring home a puppy.

Rosie had diarrhoea later that day and she made no attempt to get up before soiling herself. So they called me in the afternoon to say that after much thought they had decided to have Rosie put to sleep where she lay, unless there was any reason I could think of not to. Unless I had changed my mind and could still offer a miraculous cure.

Sadly I couldn't and I supported their brave decision. I had seen a few dogs put to sleep by this time and I offered to attend and be present if they wanted me there. The lady thanked me, but declined my offer, saying they felt they owed it to Rosie to be there for her themselves. I tried and failed to stem my tears as she spoke. What wonderful, caring people. What a terribly sickening outcome. How awful that they had left home so keen, well-prepared and excited a few days ago to find a puppy to love and care for and they had ended up in this awful situation through no fault of their own. Indeed, they had ended up in this situation *because* they were kind, caring people.

For many months the memory of Rosie's poor glazed eyes and her weak, stained body haunted me and she came to me in my dreams. Sad dreams, frustrating dreams, where I couldn't get over a fence to help her and she was crying in pain as I tried in vain to save her.

I hated my job for a while. I started to look around for something else to do. I'd had a few cruelty cases recently and those on top of the horrible, hopeless Rosie case had made me wonder if I was really cut out for this job anymore. I hadn't started working with dogs to spend time recommending that they be put to sleep. I hadn't started this work to see suffering and pain so often. I had gone into dog behaviour hoping to bring happiness, understanding and the joy of dog ownership, such that I had had with my own dogs. Sure, I knew there would be difficult days and cases, but I hadn't understood how often I would see cruelty, neglect, outright stupidity or hopelessness.

I rang the RSPCA and contacted the local dog warden to report what had happened and give the address of Rosie's former owner. There was little else I felt I could do at that time. Later I produced an article advising people how to choose a healthy puppy, from a good breeder. And I just hoped that the awful memories would slowly fade from my mind and from those of the family.

But then, one day, I had a phone call from the family again.

They had found another breeder and had decided to get the puppy they originally wanted. They had called her Rose in memory of Rosie and they wanted everything to go by the book for this puppy. Could I come round and do a private session with them, please?

And so it was that I found myself back in the little back room, but this time it was bright with sunshine and there was a host of colourful puppy toys littering the floor and a little bundle of happiness and health leaping and bounding around, filling the place with joy. This animal smelt of sweet biscuits, the way puppies do, and she was clean, bright and full of naughtiness and puppy vigour. Who could not be happy with a puppy in their living room! The family were transformed – gone were the black rings around their eyes and here were smiles and the sound of laughter. All three members of the family were giggling and grinning with joy as we sat and watched little Rose as she systematically stalked and killed her toys and then rolled over to have her tummy rubbed. As we watched I did all I could to not look at the patch of floor where months earlier I had knelt next to old Rosie. I didn't want to remember the pain she was in or the pain in my own heart; I wanted instead to focus on the new puppy and the smiles. I helped them with the pup's toilet training issues, helped them to understand how to stop her mouthing and chewing and gave them some top tips before thanking them for having faith in me enough to call me back to their home. I apologised again for not being able to help with Rosie and, my work done, started to make moves toward leaving. The family thanked me and as I stood, the mother stood with me and we went to leave the room, the kindly lady leading the way.

In the doorway of that brightly lit room, I paused and suddenly I felt the need to look back to see the puppy once more, but also to see the place where old Rosie had been lying when I last saw her. I felt the memory calling to me, her memory. I felt a kind of need to pay her respect by revisiting the memory. By feeling the pain she had felt and sharing it with her again. I felt the need to bid my own farewell to the noble animal who had suffered so. A wave of sadness hit me as if it were happening all over again. The image tore into my mind and I could even remember the smell. It took my breath away as once more the memory ripped into my emotions and raged through my body.

After a few painful moments, I pulled my eyes away from the floor and the memory and with one fleeting last glance I looked at the puppy, now deeply involved in digging a frantic hole in the rug.

But wait, what was that behind her? My heart stopped for a moment and I held my breath, as a tingle ran down my spine. Standing there in the shadow, behind the puppy in the corner of the room, I saw the shape of an older, bigger dog. A golden face with kind, soft eyes, pain-free, watching patiently over the happy puppy. It was just a shadowy form but unmistakable in its outline and I think I sensed more than felt what it was. I saw Rosie standing there. She looked peaceful, calm, happy, and well.

And then she was gone.

It seems Rosie had found her final resting place in this home and she had stayed around to do what she had done all her life: watch over and care for puppies. But this time, the place she was in was full of care, of love, and of happiness and laughter. I felt at that moment as if a circle had been completed, as if some passing had taken place and that finally I could lay to rest in my own mind the terrible memory of Rosie's last days. The nightmares about Rosie never came again.

During my career I have encountered many breeders, and of course through our puppy classes we see thousands of puppies who in their own way tell the story of the breeders who have produced them. With some of the cases I have seen it would be easy to turn against breeders on the whole. But on the flip side, I have been lucky enough to encounter and indeed buy puppies from breeders who have the welfare of their breed and the animals they produce as their highest priority. Despite my background and experience, I have been pleased to be subject to questionnaires assessing my suitability to own one of their carefully bred animals. I've had to sign contracts to say that if I can't cope with a puppy then it will be returned to the breeder. These are breeders that care and who take responsibility, for life, for their puppies. I've seen some of the efforts and research that some breeders go to in order to produce healthy, fit, well-socialised animals and give great after-sales support and advice to new owners. But sadly, I have also encountered some breeders who are not like that.

Tragically, Rosie's story is by no means an isolated or rare one. Increasingly, it seems to me, we see puppies come through class that are so poorly produced or nourished that by the time they arrive at class at anything between eight and fourteen weeks they are sick, weak, lame, or just poor specimens for their breed. I've seen pups that are meant to be one breed but are in fact another. I've seen pups who are supposed to be a certain age but are clearly not. I've seen puppies who have legs so bad that I am horrified that a breeder has sold an animal on, knowing that animal is sure to need immediate and expensive medical treatment, just to be able to continue walking. Each of these cases sickens me to the core. The heartbreak of the families involved, especially when there are children at home, when they realise their puppy is ill or needs expensive and worrying medical intervention, is a tragedy in itself.

Puppy 'farms' or 'mills' are becoming increasingly common and it is important that everyone is made aware of this. In writing this chapter I discovered to my surprise that there are still people out there who have no idea that these things go on. Whilst the animal welfare and rescue organisations do what they can to help, they are simply overwhelmed with cases. We, the general public, can do all we can to ensure that by drying up the sales of such outlets, we condemn them to failure.

Sometimes puppies reared in situations like Rosie's are sold out of 'in between' homes. People take litters from farms or mills and sell them from their kitchen at home, as if they were bred there in the home. At other times you might be offered a 'meeting' at a motorway service station or hotel car park, so you never see where the animal was bred or the conditions of its parents. An increase in popularity of the crossbreeds like the Labradoodles, Springerdors, Cockerpoos, ShihTzipoos and the others like them mean that puppies as breeds are more difficult to identify. We have puppies come through class that are called 'Labradoodles' or 'Cockerpoos' and to me it is clear that in fact they are not those breeds at all. Either that or they are a genetic throwback from long ago. Which means families that have chosen a breed after researching what fits their lives end up with a breed, or indeed size, or set of behaviour traits, that they were not expecting, or wanting.

Many breeds have genetic health problems that relate specifically to their breed. Many conscientious breeders perform routine health checks on their breeding animals in an effort to phase out the weaknesses or problems. However some who breed the popular crossbreeds appear to exempt themselves from this process, putting the animals at further risk from poor health or form.

My own puppy Karma had many medical problems, yet her breeders were good and they were open and honest with regard to everything about her. The rest of the litter were healthy individuals but little Karma seemed to carry the brunt of the problems, perhaps because she was the smallest, perhaps the runt. When Karma's various problems became more apparent, their response was to offer me another puppy, to take Karma back into their care. But I considered Karma a gift, and she surely has been. In her case, the breeders did no wrong; she just turned out wrong. Cloud too had terrible bone abnormalities that ultimately led to her early demise, but again her breeder had done the health tests and believed her to be of good stock. Things can still go wrong, even with good breeders. But it is their reaction to it that matters.

When you look for a breeder, look long and look hard before committing. Go on a friend's recommendation or that of a dog trainer (who sees more puppies than most), or from a vet who can attest to the health of a particular breeder's offspring.

There are fabulous, talented, caring breeders out there, for all different breeds. Make sure for the sake of the pup in question, your own peace of mind and pocket and that of your family, that you find one of them. Or instead choose to rescue an older dog, whose medical condition might be more obvious.

There is always a risk when buying a puppy. Any puppy can become ill or have genetic weakness or behavioural issues. But if you buy from good breeding stock, with a well-considered breeding programme and a conscientious breeder, you limit the risks that we all face.

And by doing that, we can all honour the life of Rosie, and that which she and others like her have suffered to teach us.

Run free, beautiful Rosie.

Arnie: Nowhere to Run; Nowhere to Hide

Arnie was never a 'case' dog. This is the story of one of the dumb things I got involved with during my quest for further experience and knowledge of dog training and behaviour. It may serve as a warning to others interested in dog training if they wish to avoid what happened to me!

I had found myself through an odd set of circumstances invited to an 'open demonstration day' for the families and friends of members of the British forces. It was held on an army base in Wiltshire and started at lunchtime. It was a lovely day and as I had time to kill I wandered down to the event arena in the morning to see what was being prepared and exercise my dogs at the same time. I was in luck! As I drew close I could hear the sound of barking. German Shepherd barking I knew. How exciting. The military dogs were due to do a show that afternoon and I hoped that I had discovered them practising.

Now it's true that the military often get bad press as regards dog handling and some of their training techniques and animal husbandry in general, and there have been occasions when it appears that working dogs have been treated unkindly at best and cruelly and barbarically at worst. And that is not what any of us wants to hear. But that is not always how it is – of that I am quite certain. My personal experience of such trainers has been all positive. I'd spent over two years working alongside an ex-army handler, who had an OBE for dog-training services to the Queen, and who taught me loads about sniffer dogs and obedience too. I'd also run a couple of courses with another scentwork trainer with an RAF dog handler-instructor background. Both truly brilliant trainers! In addition to that I'd had a police dog handler work with me and teach at CaDeLac for nearly two years. He adored his dogs and was kind and indeed very loving to them in every way.

I am sure there are some bad handlers and training techniques out there, but my personal experience was all good and it had also taught me a great deal. So I was looking forward to watching these guys and seeing what I could learn. Secretly, what I really wanted was to get chatting to them and maybe even get involved.

There was a low bank surrounding the event arena and seeing that there was a soldier walking out with a huge GSD as I arrived, I sat down with my dogs in the sun and began to watch and absorb, utterly fascinated. A couple more dogs and handlers arrived and there was a confab between them as their dogs lay patiently beside them. I was so looking forward to this afternoon's demo.

I watched as some guys finished building a Wendy house/ shed in one corner, as the GSD was put through his paces just to one side. He performed a number of retrieves, some nice heelwork and a down stay as his handler went off to help with the construction of the shed. Once completed, the shed looked like a miniature house with a chimney and a window. I sat transfixed as the GSD, who had lain calmly, as if enjoying the sun, was picked up out of his stay and led away by his handler. Another soldier, dressed as a vagrant and wearing a sleeve, came into the arena. He carried a wooden stick and was preparing himself to practise the afternoon's demo.

Once the GSD was positioned some distance away, the 'vagrant' started to shout at the dog and wave his stick, from a distance of perhaps a hundred yards. The dog's handler shouted for the man to drop the stick and lie on the floor. The dog began to bark and it looked very scary indeed.

The vagrant ignored the request and with a last wave of his stick and a goading call of "You can't get me!" to the dog, he turned and ran toward the shed. The dog was released and pounded after the vagrant, who reached the shed, opened the door and stepped inside, shutting the door behind him and the dog out. Or so I thought. But the dog had other ideas and he changed his line of chase and jumped clear through the window. Out of sight I could hear the dog grappling and the man shouting, "Call off your dog! Call off your dog!" The dog's handler ran to the shed and opened the door with mock caution. The dog, bum first, came slowly out of the door dragging the vagrant, held by the grab sleeve in his mouth. The dog had saved the day. Hooray for the dog!

I was very impressed and wondered, as I had many times before, whether I could get involved somehow with the training of these amazing service animals. I also thought what a great idea the pretend house had been and wondered if I could incorporate such a thing in one of our demos at work. I sat there still watching the dog, which by now had released the man and was sitting calmly at the handler's side as if nothing had happened. Then a voice came from my side.

"Hello. What lovely Collies you have, do they work?" A big soldier stood beside me.

Always blushing when someone said nice things about my dogs, I felt my face flush as I replied, "Oh, thank you. Yes, this one works sheep. Well, sort of. I was just watching that dog chasing the man into the house. I so love to see dogs work and the idea of the shed is inspired. Are you a dog handler?" The conversation flowed as I told him of my dog training history and he told me of his involvement with, and love for, the military dogs. And then it happened.

"If you're free this afternoon and looking to get involved then we could do with a volunteer in one of the demos. Would you be interested? "

Would I be interested? Are you kidding me? I felt the excitement rise inside me and without hesitation I said, "Oh yes, count me in!"

He smiled. "OK. Great. Well, at 1400 hours precisely I'd like you to stand on the second from front row of that viewing area." He waved to his right, where I could see the rope fence that separated the arena from the spectators. "You see that litter bin? Stand just to the right of that and then we will come and get you for the demo. OK?"

I agreed enthusiastically, and with that he bid me an enjoyable day and wandered off toward the dog vans parked in the shade of a large tree.

Oh, how terribly exciting! I got up and trotted off to tell everyone I knew that in the afternoon I was going to be taking part in the dog demo. I was smiling inside at the day's events. Though I didn't know what I was going to do exactly, beyond standing by the bin at a certain time, I was thrilled to be involved and I couldn't wait.

As the day wore on I got more and more excited and when the time came for the dog demo I found my place by the bin and I waited. The demo began and I saw the dog drag the man from the house, some very good precision obedience and agility exercises, and then with only five minutes left before it was my time, I could feel my stomach churning with excitement and expectation. At precisely 1400 hours the demo was in full flight and a couple of dogs were doing recalls over hurdles showing their strength and prowess, and with a tinge of disappointment I wondered if I'd been forgotten.

I stood as tall as I could and rocked gently from side to side, hoping to draw attention to myself in case the person who was being sent to collect me didn't recognise me. *Please don't forget me, please don't forget me!*

It was 1405 hours and knowing what military time precision is like, I was starting to feel glum. Perhaps it had been a wind-up? The military are good at those. Perhaps their plans had changed? I felt my face becoming gloomy.

And then I heard a minor bustle behind me and as I turned to see what was happening I saw only momentarily a huge, burly man, about 6' 2", dressed in black and wearing a balaclava, stepping down the bank towards me. I hardly had time to register what was happening before his arm was around my neck from behind and I was dragged sideways and off my feet. He held me in the grip of one single, rather huge, muscly arm, and walking backwards, he dragged me by my throat down the bank and over the ring rope into the arena.

Now if there's one thing I learnt that day it's that the military like to do demos as if they are the real thing. I don't know if he was caught up in the acting or if to him he was holding me only lightly, but from my point of view I was genuinely frightened. I could hardly breathe, such was the grip he had on my throat, and I felt completely terrified as if this was all real. Indeed I wondered if it *was* all real… Had something gone wrong and I really was being kidnapped?

He shouted out across the arena, "Don't come any closer, else I'll kill her." Had I had my feet on the ground I would have tried to get away, demo or no demo. It all felt so real. So terrifying. But I just couldn't move. He was a huge man, and with no purchase for my feet with which to lever myself I had no choice but to go with whatever he wanted me to do.

After shouting some more at the people in the arena, he leant forward and whispered into my ear, "Scream for the audience."

Scream? It was all I could do to get air into my lungs. I don't think there was any spare to let out a scream. Had there been, I already would have been screaming as loud as I could and fighting for my release. I didn't want to be in the demo anymore. But obligingly, I did my best and let out a genuine, though pathetic, whimper/scream.

My body was convinced that this was a real kidnap situation and I could feel the rush of adrenalin from the surprise and shock of the heavy-handed way I was being manoeuvred. There was nothing I could do as he dragged me backwards, further into the arena.

And then I heard someone else shout and realised what was going to happen and I thought I would surely poo my pants, and I cursed myself for having agreed to be part of this utter madness.

I heard the words "Let go of the girl or I will release the dog", and it crossed my mind that I might indeed pass out with fear.

Now having spent the morning watching those dogs, I'd seen one drag the big vagrant from the house by his arm. I knew about sleeve training and I knew the dog would be aiming for the sleeve. But I also wondered what would happen if the dog forgot to grab the sleeve, or indeed the armed man, and grabbed the girl by mistake.

So it now dawned on me that in a very few seconds I too might be experiencing one of these dogs first-hand. If you have ever been chased by a police or military dog I am sure you will know the terror I felt that moment. If you haven't, then my advice is this: do not ever break civilian law. Do not ever break military law. In fact, do not ever do anything that might incur the wrath of a military or police dog or its hander. Be nice and law-abiding always.

And then he released the dog. I couldn't see it as I had my back to it, and for that I was relieved. But I knew it had been released as the dog's barking had stopped, the shouting had stopped, my captor tightened his grip and the audience made a mass inhaling noise as the dog was let loose and came pounding towards us.

And then worse than knowing the dog was coming, worse than not being able to breathe, worse than the pain I now felt in my neck – worse than all of that – the huge man spun around and put me between him and the dog! I was facing a forty-kilo GSD in full flight, mouth open, saliva streaming as he charged towards us. German Shepherds are bulky animals and they take some time to get going into full flight. They are truly magnificent in full flight if you are simply an observer. But if, in fact, you are facing one of these incredible animals, running straight at you, then they are utterly terrifying. Particularly if they have that committed, determined, single-minded *I'm going to get you* look in their eyes. This dog, I observed weakly, was confident, fast, huge, and intent on his course of action.

As the dog drew ever closer towards us, fifty yards, forty yards, thirty yards, I could now hear his laboured breathing, panting with each stride, pushed from his body by the force of each powerful sequence of footfall. I could also hear that the man's breathing had quickened. He had done this before, no doubt, but still his grip and attitude changed as soon as the dog was in flight. He was scared too – I'm sure he must have been.

At twenty yards the sound of the dog's paws hitting the floor in four time was almost like a drum in my head, exploding my brain in terror with the rash huffing of his galloping breath. Everything went into slow motion as my captor pushed me further still toward the oncoming dog.

I was now resigned to death. I had been sweating for a while and could feel it trickling down my arms as I flailed to free myself now that my feet were momentarily back on the floor. Such were those last few seconds that it seemed like an eternity. I wondered if anyone would think to feed my dogs tonight, after I had died. I wondered who might come to my funeral, after I had died. I wondered how much of me there might be left after the attack. How messy it would be. I was only wearing shorts and a tee shirt. I saw the dog adjust his stride to make his final strike and then with the last footfall of his chase, it seemed he leapt straight at me, as my captor thrust me forward to face the dog, as if I were an unwanted rag doll. With an incredible display of power the huge, slavering dog took off with a roar, and I thought that this was my last moment of summer. Of anything. I saw the dog's mouth, wide open, come towards me. I saw his glistening teeth as I closed my eyes and awaited the terrible impact. But all I felt was the back of one paw brush past me and I heard and felt the thud as the dog grabbed the man's sleeve. I was released at once as the dog grabbed the man who held me and with the force of the full gallop, the dog took the kidnapper clean off his feet and pinned him to the floor.

It seemed I'd been thrown aside at the last moment and I hit the floor with a thud, shocked, terrified, exhausted and thankful that I was still alive. I watched from a few feet away as the dog snarled and bit and pulled at the sleeve the man was wearing and waited for the "Out" call to come from his handler. The moment it did, the dog, with one last shake as if to make a point, released the man and trotted back to his handler as if nothing had happened. The audience, breathing again, as I was, erupted into applause and the dog, panting heavily from his exertions, sat down at his handler's side. My captor righted himself and got up on his feet, and reaching out for my arm he pulled me from the floor and held my hand high in the air, signalling to the audience to clap for me, the girl hero of the tale.

I had dog slobber all down my side and I was sweating profusely; my knees were shaking and I was touching each arm with the other hand trying to work out if all my limbs were there. I checked my throat to see if my head was still attached as usual.

My captor leant over and whispered, "Well done!" in my ear and the dog handler nodded at me with an admiring, knowing look and a wry smile.

I staggered a bit and then I looked at the dog. The dog, who only seconds before had been pounding flat out toward me, had a doggy smile on his face. I'm sure he wagged his tail at me, as if to say, "That was fun, wasn't it?" And the soldiers got on with their demo, taking the dog with them. Arnie – his name, I later found out – had been grabbing the sleeve for a few years now. Apparently he had only ever got the wrong person once, I was assured sheepishly.

It was that evening and I was in the bar with friends when I recognised the huge man, who had been my captor earlier that day, by the size of his arms. Having removed his balaclava, he now came over and offered to buy me a drink. As he went to the bar, I studied the size of the guy and recalled how utterly incapacitated I had been by only one of his arms. My breathing quickened perceptibly as I relived the experience in a moment. He returned from the bar armed with two glasses and placing them on the table, sat down next to me. I was still in shock and I felt I would never be the same person again, but I was still trying to look cool. I thanked him for the drink and put the glass to my lips, as if everything was normal, as if I hadn't nearly died that day.

As he spoke I turned to face him. "You did real well today. Did you enjoy it?"

I spurted out the drink I had just supped and it hit him

square in the chest. Enjoy it? Was he serious? I looked at the wet patch on his shirt and felt embarrassed, but somewhat justified.

He glanced down briefly at his now-wet shirt before continuing, unfazed. Presumably this had happened to him before. "Only if you're around, we have another demo next week about seventy miles from here and it looks so much better with a girl in the kidnap scene. We wondered if you might like to help us out again, as no one ever wants to be the girl." Oh really? You don't say!

Not wanting to lose face I politely declined, telling him that I was sorry but I already had something on that weekend. "Otherwise I would have loved to!" I lied.

I was too young to die!

Lucky Spots

In dogs, there are naughty spots and lucky spots. This is a story of a dog with both. A dog called Spots.

This was one of my very first cases from when I had just started out in dog behaviour professionally. It kind of set the scene for the work I was to take on, or so I thought. It's odd – these days most of the behaviour work we get is 'aggression', though it doesn't always turn out to be aggression. But mostly people ring saying their dogs are either aggressive to people, or dogs, or both. I'm not exactly sure what has happened to the other sorts of cases – the unusual, fun, or easy ones. There don't seem to be so many of those anymore. I wonder why?

Anyway. When the call came in I was very inexperienced in terms of professional consultations and not that busy either, so I just took the case without asking too many questions.

She said in a good-natured way, "Hello, I have heard you are good with dogs and I have a problem with my dog. No matter what I do, the darned dog won't come back and I don't have time to stand around and wait it out anymore. Can you come and see me as soon as possible, please?" She was light-hearted and pleasant, but authoritative. So I agreed. These days I would have asked a couple of questions and suggested what I eventually suggested for this case, solving it over the phone, but back then I was just curious and keen to see the dog. And indeed, this assertive lady.

So because of my lack of experience, I went to the dog's home instead of resolving the case on the phone. And I am so glad I did.

She gave me directions and I knew vaguely where it was. About thirty miles from me and in a part of the country I had ridden in as a child. It held lovely memories of the smell of hot pony, hot rider and wonderful, well-oiled leather. A nice lady, in a lovely place, a great sunny day and a fun road journey to boot. I set off that afternoon. I was keen. Excited. And broke.

As I turned into the little driveway I could see nothing but huge wooden gates in front of me. There was a buzzer, and I positioned myself to press it from the car window. I buzzed, said my name and as the gates very slowly began to open, a whole new world opened up to me. Literally. As the gates drew back I saw the drive curve around to the right, but immediately in front of me was a huge valley with open land this side and on the other, an ancient woodland coiled its way up the hillside above the green meadows. A wide stream tumbled and fell along the bottom of the valley. It was enchanting. It smelt of summer and country smells.

I drove along the top of one side of the valley, all the way looking down at the beautiful scene below my car. I looked for the house and I couldn't see it, such was the length of the drive, but eventually after a few minutes, it came into view. It was like a fairy-tale castle-cum-manor house-cum-stately home. It had a *huge* entrance foyer that I imagined horses and carriages must once have pulled up in.

Under the stone arches of the massive entrance porches a smiling boy, around ten, stood waving happily at me. As I drew closer he began to shout loudly, "Mummy, Spots' new doctor is here. Mummy, she is here!" It made me smile that I had been 'promoted' to dog doctor.

Soon after, his mother, sister and their housekeeper

appeared. His mother strode forward on heeled boots and held out her tanned hand, giving mine a good firm shake as she smiled at me, nodded and told me she was so delighted to meet me and thank goodness I was able to come so quickly.

"What a stroke of good luck!" she said. It certainly was.

But as for the errant Spots the Dalmatian, after the polite hellos there came a crashing sound from behind. We turned to see, appearing from an old barn, with straw and some kind of sticky black goo all over his head, a very happy-looking Spots the dog, who oddly had a plastic bucket dangling from his neck, which as he squeezed through the barn door had made the crashing sound which had alerted us to his impending, rather dramatic, but joyful arrival. All smiling, all excited and all very pleased to see me, he bounded toward me with an enthusiasm I expected to knock me off my feet.

At the sight of the bucket the children giggled happily and their mother, also smiling, exclaimed, "Oh, Spots, you are such a naughty boy. What have you been up to now?" I caught Spots by the collar as he leapt and jumped at me enthusiastically and between us we managed to free him of the bucket. Spots by this time had smelt the liver cake in my pocket and as we walked toward the house he trotted at my side, sniffing enthusiastically. The lady of the house noticed and said, "I can't believe he is coming in with you now. Perhaps you should come live here with us!" I wish!

As we began to talk, I discovered that the habit of the family in the summer months was to go riding after breakfast each morning, along the valley one side, crossing the little stream at its narrow head by the spring, and then back through the woods, along the long meadows and then jumping back over the stream at the narrow bit where the smallest pony could manage to jump, then back to the stable yard, and for the children their schooling then began. They were tutored at home by a number of teachers. The problem with Spots was described. He was brilliant when out riding with them each morning. He ran alongside jumping the same things the horses did, occasionally breaking off to chase after a rabbit here and there. Having a lot of fun and making them all laugh, sometimes, with his antics. He was brilliant whilst they rode; he kept a safe distance from the horses, but stayed close, and was undaunted by any terrain and any weather.

The trouble was that when they got back to the stables next to the house, Spots would not come back into the house. They had a terrible job with him running around, playing hide and seek with them, until sometimes the children were almost late for their lessons, I was told. The gardener had once spent four hours trying to get him in, in the rain. He stayed just out of reach and couldn't be caught and sometimes he just wouldn't go into the house at all.

"He is a little blighter of a dog," she said. She smiled as she said it. What a lovely family: a delightful dog, enchanting home, wonderful way of life. I felt so pleased for them that they had all they had. They just kept laughing and smiling with one another about how flipping naughty that dog was! Lucky people. Lucky, really nice people. I decided there and then to try to be a nicer person, in case it made me that lucky.

I looked at Spots and it was clear that he was in top health. His eyes were bright and clear; his muscles rippled down his back legs. I'd felt the muscles in his chest and could see the muscle on top of his head, indicating that he was quite probably a bone-eater, which in those days many dogs were. He oozed peak physical fitness. He smelt sweet and clean and he looked very, very happy. What a lucky dog!

I asked about his lifestyle. What was in a typical day for him?

It didn't take many seconds to discover the potential problem.

"We feed him his food in the morning, we put his biscuits in to soak and then we eat. Spots waits while we eat and then whatever is left from our plates goes into his bowl. Sometimes it's bacon and sometimes it's porridge but he always eats it all up. He's a greedy dog," she told me.

"How much of his daily ration does he eat in the morning?" I enquired.

"All of it."

I had hoped that I could spend all day questioning them, just to spend time in this wonderful fairy-tale life – people really lived like this! Wow! But sadly it wasn't to be. We had gone straight to the root cause of the problem.

I was further advised that after their morning ride they had tried to use treats to tempt Spots into the house, but to no avail. The normally greedy Spots, who had been known to steal a few things off the kitchen worktops and occasionally raid the bin, was having none of this luring him in with food business!

I began to explain to them.

Dogs, being predators, are designed to hunt (running, jumping), then catch and kill, and then eat their meal. After eating it would be normal for a dog to sleep off the exercise and the meal. That is the natural, normal order of things: run, eat, sleep. It is the healthy order of things. In Spots' life, it was all the wrong way round. He was eating his meal and then with a full stomach was running and jumping as he went out on the ride. Running around on a full stomach is not that healthy anyway for any dog, and it is thought that exercise on a full stomach is a contributing factor to some cases of 'bloat', a serious, life-threatening condition that had taken the life of many I had known, and that particularly affects deep-chested dogs, like Spots. So, it wasn't healthy for him, and not helpful at providing him with an incentive to return indoors after the ride. Hence why luring with treats wouldn't work: he was already full of food!

The young boy interjected with a smile, no doubt remembering the image in his head, saying that Spots was such a greedy dog that when his food bowl was filled he nearly "wagged his tail right off". I smiled inside as I heard Spots' enthusiasm described this way.

So before continuing I decided to perform a test, to see if my plan might work. I asked the little boy to go to the room where the dog food was kept and put some food in Spots' bowl, and then to place it on the side where they normally left it to soak. The little lad bounded off happily and Spots, who lay peacefully on his bed, looked up as the boy left the kitchen and opened the utility door – the dog food door. As the boy dropped some biscuits into Spots' bowl, he leapt up and I saw for myself how he did indeed look like he might wag his tail right off. It made me smile again.

Leaving the bowl on the side as they did each morning, the little lad returned to us and the conversation continued. Spots was now looking from the utility door to us, clearly reminding us that they had forgotten to give him the bowl. This, I was told, was how he always behaved. And this was exactly what I wanted to hear.

I observed an interesting and pleasing thing in this family as we chatted. The housekeeper, the gardener and the children were all in attendance and they all chipped in happily and with smiles, and with tales of Spots and his various doggy antics. The love for their dog was clear, as was the love they had for each other. My mind drifted as I wondered vaguely if it was the love they shared that made them so happy or the happiness that made them so loving. Each time one spoke, the others stopped to listen. Even the youngest child was given respect for her view and time to express it. Again I marvelled at the joy of this family and the way they conversed.

I offered my advice. Tomorrow, before the ride, they were to prepare Spots' food as normal. But then instead of giving it to him, they were to place it on the kitchen counter and then go out riding. I was hoping that Spots would remember the food had been left behind and having not been fed, be keener to come into the house after the ride.

I was unsure if this would work, but I figured it was worth a go and I explained that if it didn't work I had other ideas which I could relay over the phone to them, with no further charge to them.

The following day Spots' owner called me. Again her happiness and enthusiasm shone through and her words made me smile.

"Hello, it's Spots' mum from yesterday." Excitement was evident in her voice. "You are a miracle-worker." This sounded good! "We did as you said and put Spots' bowl of food on the side before riding. He didn't want to leave it, so we had to hold his collar to get him out to go outside. Once we were out he was OK, but on the way back, Spots ran off ahead. He was there at the door when we got home, wagging his tail. Wanting his food. You are so clever!"

It had worked perfectly. Everybody was happy. Spots was healthier for being fed *after* his exercise and he was coming straight back into the house, where they wanted him to be.

And I was a better person for having met such a lovely family and their lovely, very spotty dog, Spots.

A few weeks later I called to see how things were going with Spots. Everything was fine. Spots was routinely waiting at the door once they returned to the house. Everyone was happy and at such an early stage of my behaviour career I was delighted to have been recommended to them. I felt I was in the right place at the right time.

Little did I know what was to happen next…

Can't See the Wood for the Trees

These days I am often surprised at how an owner can be completely oblivious to something that to me is staring us all right in the face. There are countless times when someone relays the tale of their dog's behaviour and I am left thinking, but hopefully not saying out loud, is this a wind up? Can you not see what is happening there to make that happen?

When this happens I try to remember a few very important things. Firstly, it is far more difficult to see what is creating an issue, or indeed how to resolve it, if you are 'in there' with the issue. Or if you are unwittingly adding to or contributing to that issue. Or indeed if you are looking in the wrong direction. You can only see what's there if you are looking at all aspects of a situation and often it's very difficult to do that! It is too easy to become prejudiced into thinking that a behaviour is based on something you already know, understand, have read about or seen. But dogs are much more complicated than we currently understand them to be, of that I am quite certain.

A classic example of a person unwittingly creating a situation is when someone says their dog gets over-excited at the door before a walk and then is a nightmare on the lead. It screams or whines and barks and spins and can't be calmed. Often, though not always, this is as a result of a member of the household 'winding the dog up' before a walk from an early age.

Investigation into the dog's background often reveals some or all of the following immediately prior to the walk. "Do you wanna go for a walk?" The dog perks up and stares at the owner. "Do you?" Excitement in their voice. The dog stands and his tail wags. "Walkies?" Higher pitched. The dog is now up and at the door, wagging its tail. "You wanna go walkiiiieeess?" The dog whines and then utters a bark. The human acts excited and smiles. "Waaallkies!" The dog leaps and begins to bark. The owner reaches for the lead; the dog's excitement mounts. They put on the lead and go to the door, the dog leaps toward it, revved up and ready for action. "Let's go!" They are now both shouting in their excitement and together they launch joyfully into the world beyond the door, barking, leaping, whining, spinning, jumping and lunging forward.

Later when the owner decides that the excitement at the door is getting out of hand, especially now the dog is fully grown and weighs nearly as much as they do and the jumping up is causing the owner to unbalance and the barking is incessant until the door is opened, and then the leaping and barking continues well into the walk – then the owner decides that they don't want their dog to do that anymore and they ring for help. Sometimes they have a vague inkling that their own behaviour has caused it and sometimes they genuinely are oblivious.

When I get these calls I try to remember this story. It taught me so much about myself and how my view of the world affects what I can and cannot see. And in that memory holds the key to staying open to the fact that obvious things are not always that obvious to everyone.

One day when I was out walking Cassie and Lace, Lace

suddenly did something she had never done before, as is the way with every new behaviour; there is a first time for everything. Because it was a brand new behaviour and it all happened so fast, I was surprised and didn't know what to do, and by doing nothing I therefore endorsed it.

We were walking along, everyone was minding their own business and calm, and we had passed a few dog walkers. Cassie made friends with a few of the dogs, but Lace as usual minded her own business and no one really bothered her. Lace was never a dog to go make friends or play with dogs; mostly she just ignored them and them her.

And then one day, without any reason that I could determine, Lace suddenly went from sniffing the grass to roaring and charging toward a young, small Spaniel-type dog a few metres away. For a few seconds she seemed genuinely angry as if the dog had committed some heinous crime against her. She bared her teeth and flew at the dog for no reason that I could determine. The dog had been trotting as if to pass us, its owner trailing behind, and it appeared to me to be utterly focused on something beyond us and of no threat to Lace or me. She chased it a few metres and then stopped, returning instantly to what she had been doing, as if nothing had happened. Meanwhile the dog, now wary of her, scampered off, looking back briefly with a worried look on its face.

Surprised by her unusual and out-of-character behaviour I apologised to the owner and said words that these days I hear nearly every day from dog owners: "Sorry. She has never done that before!" Well, she hadn't.

The owner smiled and waved her hand with a dismissive, "Oh, dogs will be dogs!" I heaved a sigh of relief that the lady wasn't angry with Lace or with me.

Over the next few years, with enough 'gaps' between events to make me think that Lace's worrying behaviour was a one-off, or later a two-off, three, four, five, six or seven-off, Lace kept doing the same thing: chasing dogs off for no particular reason that I could determine. By about the seventh time over a period of a couple of years, I had stopped gaping incredulously at her, flabbergasted and fascinated at the same time, and I had got off my backside and decided that I must stop it. I had shouted, "Leave it!" and called her away and she had responded instantly and left the dog. As long as I saw it coming I could halt it immediately, I realised. If I didn't see it coming and she took me by surprise, it took maybe a second for me to react and call her away. She always came instantly. But mostly I didn't see it coming. On no occasion did she make any physical contact and no harm had ever come of the behaviour, but it was an ugly thing to see and it perturbed me deeply that I couldn't understand or indeed predict it.

As no contact was made, it all seemed just to be a chasing bluff designed to set the other dog running away but not to cause any harm. Most owners were, as the first had been, dismissive and accepting of the quirks of dog behaviour. Some, however, were understandably quite cross and I found myself apologising a lot because I just never saw it coming. Lace, in full flight, teeth bared and roaring, was an intimidating sight and though she never touched the other dogs, ever, she did look very scary. Even to me!

On each occasion I was totally perplexed, worried and spent a long time pondering the situation. At first I thought it was quite likely that she had taken a dislike to other bitches, but not male dogs. It is more common for dogs of both sexes to have run-ins with dogs of their own sex. Maybe that was it? But by dog number three she had proved me wrong and chased a male dog. After each incident, I would keep her on lead for a few days when around other dogs, but the behaviour disappeared and naively I thought it had 'gone'. Curiously, she encountered hundreds of dogs out walking that she didn't do this to.

Then I decided it was young dogs she targeted. Many older dogs will tell off adolescent dogs that are overly boisterous and it was true that some dogs that she had chased were rather frantic and out-of-control-looking animals. Telling off younger dogs, although not always pretty, is in fact normal and necessary behaviour for many dogs. Dogs need to have boundaries provided to them and older dogs can be brilliant at teaching them. But some were not younger dogs, so I threw that idea out of the window and kept searching for an answer.

On one occasion she encountered a dog several metres away deeply engrossed in sniffing a bush, not even noticing her or me, and she suddenly took off after that one. Her roar alerted the dog to her impending arrival and off it shot.

I spent many, many hours trying to work it out. Was it their colour? Nope? Their behaviour? Nope. Their size? Their sex? Nope. Was it just some locations in which she did it? Was it their age? Something I was doing? Nope. Territorial aggression? Resource-guarding? Obnoxious behaviour from the other dog? Fear aggression? Rage syndrome? Sexual conflict? Nope. Was she in pain? The vet said nope.

Well, what the heck was it then?

Deeply troubled, but unable to come up with a reason why she chose the dogs she did, I thought instead about why she *didn't* target some dogs. Perhaps the answer lay there. The dogs she didn't target numbered in the hundreds so it was a huge undertaking to observe every single dog we encountered. But I did it anyway as best I could as I didn't know what else to do, and the not knowing was driving me crazy. What was it about them? I went through the same list. Age, sex, colour, size, behaviour, location, speed, movement?

This was the days before the internet and freely available

information, so I reread books I'd already read and ordered some new ones and read those. In those days I was routinely reading every day about dog behaviour and had already acquired many dozens of books, which I pored over. But nowhere did I find anything like the behaviour I was seeing in my own dog. None of my dog friends understood it either. I began spending more time in dog-populated places just to watch what it was that Lace looked at when she encountered another dog to see if I could determine why she was doing it. But I couldn't. I took notes and I started a diary of what dogs she had been fine with and what dogs she had wanted to chase. Nothing seemed to fit. No matter how much I looked at the target dogs or the non-target dogs, I couldn't find an answer.

By this time I was in my first years of running CaDeLac and was running both agility and obedience classes as well as having increasing numbers of people come to me for help with their dog's behaviour. Overall, I was mostly successful in resolving behaviour problems, but still I couldn't find an understanding of my own dog's behaviour and it bothered me almost continually. It was like a bee in my bonnet. It couldn't rest until I had resolved it. I berated myself with thoughts like, *What kind of dog trainer can't solve a problem with their own dog?* Of course now I realise that the most difficult problems to resolve are the problems with your own dogs. When you are in it, it is very hard to 'see it'.

By this time, Cassie had sadly crossed the Rainbow Bridge and I had just Lace and my youngest dog, Cloud, who came to me as my first puppy and had now reached adolescence. As with most dogs, the onset of adolescence brought about behavioural changes in Cloud as she made the transition from puppy to adult. And one day, when we were out walking, Cloud did the exact same thing as Lace had done!

Completely out of the blue, Cloud too just targeted a dog

and sent it packing. Oh no! Disaster. What was going on? What was I to do?

Where Lace had roared and bared her teeth, young Cloud had yet to learn such communication skills, and instead she just flew in at high speed, heading straight for the dog's head, and the dog, reading her intent, just turned and fled in the opposite direction, whereupon Cloud totally disengaged and wandered off as Lace had done previously, the act seemingly finalised.

What on earth was going on?

The trouble I had now was that whilst Lace was highly responsive and trained and could easily be called away, Cloud was an adolescent, a monster and the strongest-willed and most determined dog that I had ever and probably will ever know. She was at that time beyond my calling her off the other dog. She just ignored me. But still there was no contact made and no ill feelings after from either dog. Nor did most owners seem to mind.

The same pattern emerged. I kept Cloud on a lead; the behaviour disappeared. Then, feeling more confident as she had no run-ins with dozens of dogs, I let her off again. And then, out of the blue, she did it again.

But one day it was different. This time a strange thing happened. The dog was about thirty metres away and was tearing around like a lunatic. Cloud was pottering about when suddenly she stood stationary for a second and observed the manic dog.

Reading her interest in the other dog, I called for her to "Leave it" and return to me. She ignored me, watched the dog for a second longer and then she flew at it. I called to her once more, she ignored me again, and then running faster than the now fleeing dog, she overtook it and leaning her body in toward it, she pushed into it, as if to turn it. She ran past one side of the dog and began to turn it in a specific direction. (Years later I saw her do the same thing with a flock of sheep that she was being trained on.) She turned the dog away with her own body and when the dog had altered its direction, seemingly to Cloud's satisfaction, she disengaged and carried on minding her own business.

The young dog, now shocked and surprised by Cloud's behaviour (and she wasn't alone there!), fled to its owner. Once again, embarrassed at not understanding my own dog's behaviour, I turned to apologise to the owner. As I did I saw that the little 'target' dog was jumping up its owner's legs, clearly worried and wanting to be picked up. The owner grabbed the little dog and lifted it up off the floor. I was worried the owner would be angry.

But as she put it under one arm she turned, smiling at me, and said, "Thank goodness for your dog!" She waved her free hand higher in the air for me to see her own dog's lead. The little dog's collar was still attached to the lead. "She slipped her collar, the blighter. It's a good job your dog came along. I might never have caught her!"

Whilst she was clearly very pleased with Cloud's behaviour, I was puzzled. Why on earth had Cloud done this? Cloud couldn't have known the little dog had slipped her collar, could she? I dismissed it as a stupid idea. Could she have known that the dog was not going to recall and was sending it back to its owner?

Tick, tick, tick. Cogs start turning. I had a vivid memory of the dog with its head in the bushes, years ago, that Lace had chased. Its owner had been calling it.

Had the other owners been calling their dogs? I tried to remember. But I couldn't be sure either way. I hadn't noticed.

Had my dogs learnt to chase dogs back to their owners if they had been called but hadn't responded? Certainly they had barked when at training classes a dog was meant to be doing recall but had chosen instead to run around the room, inciting a riot among the other dogs.

Was it the case that my dogs, without any training from me, had learnt to help other owners retrieve their dogs when the dogs had ignored their recall command?

Could it be so? Could it be that I had focused *for so many years and for so many hours* on my main interest of *dog behaviour, to the complete exclusion of what the target dog's* owner *was doing?*

Were the random attacks not at all random? Were they in fact a very keen and fascinating observation on the part of my dogs?

Could it be that I had been blind to the single common denominator in nearly every single case of my dogs chasing other dogs?

It was indeed the case!

I tested it on my friends' dogs. Years later, Connor started to do and still does the exact same thing. Sometimes he will allow a single failed recall attempt, but if the owner calls again he will set the dog running toward its owner before completely disengaging and forgetting about it. Sometimes he will be saying a polite and friendly 'hello' to a dog and then the owner calls and he will immediately roar at it and chase it back to its owner. It looks to all intents and purposes like he has gone from Dr Jekyll to Mr Hyde, like he has flipped out and gone from friendly to horrid. But in reality he is just pushing the dog back to its owner.

I suppose for dogs like mine that see hundreds or thousands of dogs being taught recall, it is an obvious way for them to get involved and 'help'.

The error I had made was that I had spent all those years looking for an explanation by way of the behaviour of my dogs and the 'target' dogs to the exclusion of the blindingly, or more specifically audibly, obvious. I had totally missed the owners' involvement.

It was a hugely important lesson for me and I am happy to pass it on to everyone who owns a dog whose behaviour they do not understand: *In many cases of dog behaviour, maybe even most cases, what the human is doing or not doing is often the most significant thing.*

So when trying to evaluate the cause of a dog's behaviour, remember to look not just at the dogs involved, but at what the human is doing. Odd really, because it is something I normally do – look at the owner's behaviour when I am assessing dogs. But in this case, perhaps because I was so absorbed in this thing I didn't understand about my own dogs, I just didn't notice the owners' recall command fail. But my dogs did.

These days, when people say to me that their dog has done this, that or the other for no reason at all, I think to myself, *He did it for a reason that we have yet to identify. But let's look in every direction for an explanation and work on it from there.* Sometimes a cause can't be found and one can only treat symptoms. But as long as we look with an open mind, and look in every direction, for long enough and hard enough, then hopefully we will find what we are looking for.

Even if the answer is found in surprising ways.

It is now my strong belief that a lot of behaviours we see in dogs are the dogs' attempt to 'help'. I've seen it so many times, such as when observing sheepdog trials. When a dog is working sheep in a public domain where there are other sheepdogs watching at the edge of the field, it is common for several of the watching dogs to suddenly go from relaxed to 'wanting to be involved'. If you watch closely you'll see that as the outsiders take an interest in suddenly wanting to get involved it can often coincide with the moment that the dog under test, working the sheep, either tires perceptibly or loses control of the sheep; sheepdogs can determine, by watching, whether the dog working the sheep has them under control or not. When they see a dog lose control they sometimes try to jump the fence, or bark or become agitated, clearly wanting to get involved. When they see it going wrong, some of them want to put it right.

Luckily Connor, like Lace before him, is highly controllable, so if these days he does chase a dog then I usually call him off. But when a dog is doing something that endangers its own life or upsets someone or something and I believe that the owner would be better having their dog back sooner rather than later, I allow him to chase them back. He never makes contact. And usually the owners are just pleased their dog came back.

I now wonder how many other seemingly random behaviours that dogs display actually have a perfectly good explanation that humans have yet to understand. If only we could see it. I am sure there is much still to discover about dogs, and the prospect excites and enthrals me. So keep an eye on your dog. Maybe other dogs do this too? Maybe they are not doing something seemingly randomly aggressive or bolshie, but instead are performing a clever and helpful task that in its own way educates and keeps safe other people and dogs.

Dogs are so clever, so amazing and still even now, so often misunderstood.

There is a lot more to them than we have even begun to understand.

So let's keep watching, let's keep listening and let's keep an open mind always.

A Lesson Learned – the Hard Way!

Life most certainly is a journey. And it seems to me to be littered with learning moments that can fix a belief system, until something comes along to counter that belief system. By 'belief system' I mean that something has influenced us to think a certain way about something. We believe that our view is complete and correct when in fact the information we are basing our view on is incomplete, misleading, or inadequate to fully establish the facts.

For instance, when I was young I had no political beliefs because I had no knowledge or understanding of politics. Then years later, when I still had no knowledge of the subject, I was advised that I should have a political belief because I was old enough to vote; that people had died trying to win me the right to vote and that I should respect this and vote as a gesture of support for their efforts. This was sufficient motivation for me to adopt a political view, so I listened to my parents on this. They liked one party and vehemently disliked another. Their party was represented by the colour I liked the most, so that was enough information for me to form a belief system. So if anyone ever asked me, I'd say that this party was the best. Thankfully no one ever asked me to justify this!

This is a story in which something I believed to be true got me into a lot of trouble.

Cassie. My first second-hand dog. Scared of everything –
even sheep!

My baby girl Cloud. The most extraordinary dog I have ever known.

Cloud up a tree.

Cloud cooling down.

Lace. The face that everyone wanted to stroke –
still beautiful here at age 19.

Sabre's first group walk, seven days after treatment for
severe reactivity to dogs.

Mirk – yummy bone.

Sabre, the gorgeous boy
that changed all our lives
for the better.

Connor, the most handsome
dog in the world.

Mirk's love affair with beds. "Any bed will do".

The van years. Brrrrr. So cold. But we survived – just!

Happy days, best friends together.

Below: Lace and a
very young Cloud.

Van Life isn't always bad.
On an adventure on Skye, Scotland.

Baby Karma's First
trip in the van.

Connor needed a new best friend and so little
Karma came to live with us.

Me and Connor – best friends again.

Connor and Karma – their first holiday together.

It's never too late to live happily ever after.

Thanks to Barefoot Photographer (@Barefoot_IOS).

After my experience with Ben (See Chapter on Sabre), the friend's Border Collie who had barked and lunged at sheep, I had become aware that some dogs get very excited when they see sheep. So when I got Cassie, the first dog I actually could call mine, I was crucially aware that I must assess her interest in sheep and other livestock; I had read it in books. As soon as she was fit enough, Cassie and I began walking together, for several hours every day, and several more hours at weekends. I needed to establish that she was stock-proof.

One day we came across a field of sheep with lambs of around four weeks old, and the map I was following advised me that the public path went through the middle of the sheep field. The sheep, with their lambs at foot, were scattered loosely around the field and were some way off the path so I felt I could go through without disturbing them too much. Cassie was rather nervous of the sheep; she hovered behind my legs as if trying to use me as a barrier between her and them. The sheep seemed unfazed by Cassie and with only a few curious looks, moved gently away from our line of passage through the grassy field. She had her tail lowered but not between her legs, and she was kind of tiptoeing. It seemed to me that she was trying to pretend she wasn't there. I've seen many dogs do this since, and I've seen a few people do it too! It seemed to me that Cassie was more scared of the sheep than the sheep were of her.

Then, when we had nearly crossed the field, we followed the path behind some gorse bushes. Coming out from the bushes we came across a ewe with twins, grazing. As soon as we saw her, the ewe looked up and almost immediately there was a hardening of her attitude. I had never seen a sheep do this before. She stood tall on her front legs, her head raised. She looked quite scary for a cute, fluffy sheep. She stamped a front foot repeatedly on the ground, making a surprisingly loud thudding noise, in what looked like a clear warning to me: *Stay away*. She lowered her head and took some protesting steps toward us, in a mock chase, stamping her feet and protecting her lambs. As she bleated they ran to her side and she again stood and stamped her foot. This was new to me but it was clear to both me and Cassie that she wanted us to be gone. So, always obliging, Cassie turned and fled as the ewe took steps toward us, taking me with her in her fear. I had been watching the ewe and I overbalanced as Cassie led my retreat, dragging me on her lead. When I had righted myself I glanced around to see if there was anyone who had seen my embarrassing, off-balanced retreat. I smiled and thought, *Well, Cassie isn't much of a sheep-chaser. She is really frightened of sheep. She is not a brave dog.*

That is what I read from that situation. At that time in my life, that was my belief about my dog.

After that, we walked a lot in the Peak District where there are many sheep and on every occasion, she had turned her head away from the sheep as soon as we encountered them. She had tried to hide behind my legs, sometimes puling me on her lead to get away from the sheep. She had been reluctant to go into fields where sheep were, and if given a choice she would always walk on the far side of any sheep. Sheep, it seemed, worried her.

In every encounter we had with sheep, or indeed farm animals in general, I discovered Cassie wanted to stay well clear of them. I was relieved. I kept her on the lead mainly to make sure she didn't run away when we encountered sheep. By that time in my life I had come to rely on the attitude and behaviour of animals to guide me. People still baffled me. But it seemed to me that the sheep were unafraid of her and she was scared of them. I needed to keep her safe, on a lead at all times, so that she didn't run away.

A year later I was walking with Cassie in a place we had not been before, again, following the public path on a map. It was a lovely walk along a flat bit of a valley, perhaps a hundred yards wide, with a small but deep cut and a steep drop down to a powerful stream cutting through it, with boggy bits extending a few metres or so each side of the fast-flowing water course. On the far side of the valley, the flat flood land halted and the land became good pasture and rose in a steep, rounded fashion up toward the sky. On our side of the water there were trees edging the flat-bottomed valley. I could see clearly for a long way, and so Cassie had been let off lead. She was a few metres away, sniffing and rolling and enjoying the long walk just as much as I. She was easy to walk: never far away, highly responsive, happy but calm, friendly with all dogs and people she knew. She avoided those she didn't. I had already spotted some sheep way up on top of the hill ahead of us and well over a mile away. I realised as we proceeded down the valley that even when we drew level with the sheep, they would still be about a quarter of a mile away, up the hill. But I decided to put her on the lead anyway.

You just never know what might happen!

We carried on enjoying each other's company, Cassie trotting happily at my side, when I heard a commotion and looked up to where the sheep were. And then I saw something I had never seen before. The sheep were picking up speed rapidly and panic was clearly spreading among them. Behind them as they ran and sometimes running right into the middle of them, was a leggy sand-coloured dog I thought to be a Lurcher. The dog was running behind them and would then run amongst them, splitting the flock apart, and then the packet it was chasing would split again and there were just sheep running everywhere. They headed up the hill in fragmented little packets and when they reached the hedge at the top they split in either direction as the dog dived amongst them. The shape the flock made reminded me of milk splashed on a hard floor, with arms of white spreading out from the central blob.

Even from this distance it was clear that the sheep were fleeing in utter panic, and were racing back and forth at the top of the hill, terrified.

"Noooooooo!" I yelled as loud as I could, the words coming from nowhere. The Lurcher-like dog was way too far away and too involved with the sheep to hear a stranger calling out a command it might not even know.

It was one of those situations that I had never encountered before, and suddenly I had no idea what to do, but I felt I had to do something. Perhaps if I could get closer I could tie Cassie up and go into the field and somehow catch the running dog, or chase it away? I remembered years earlier when I had encountered a fox chasing chickens in a garden. It was just like that. The chickens had squawked and fled in panic from the fox, just like the sheep were from the dog. I had run at the fox, waving my arms and shouting, and had banged my hands on my thighs. Somehow I had managed to run between the fox and the chickens and frightened by this mad woman, shouting and waving, the fox had run off and some of the chickens were saved. I thought maybe if I could just get there I could do the same with the dog; somehow separate him from the sheep and chase him away. I looked up the hill and realised both the distance and the steep incline beyond the valley floor were against me, were difficult and would be time-consuming, but I had to try!

There was no time to waste, so I turned to my left and Cassie and I ran side by side toward the muddy rift in the ground that preceded the water we must cross. She was boinging happily and seemed invigorated by my sudden change of speed. I was not sure of what I might do when I got to the sheep, but I figured I'd think of something whilst I ran. I needed to help the sheep! As I ran I threw back one arm and freed myself from the heavy rucksack I had been carrying, then deftly swapped the lead into the other hand and freeing the other arm, let the rucksack fall to the ground. I heard my flask smash as it hit the floor, but that was not important, I must get to the sheep!

We reached the edge of the flat land and I looked down uncertainly at the route ahead of me. I had to face the boggy stream and I was in walking boots, not wellies. This was sucking mud. I looked at Cassie. She too was contemplating the drop down into the mud and the stream ahead. I could see that whatever happened I was going to struggle with this bit. So as I tried to see a safe way across I decided that I would manage easier without Cassie on a lead as she might choose a different path and pull me over. So, seeing that she didn't appear to be scared of the sheep at this distance, and that she was keen to progress down the drop into the mud, I let her off the lead so that I could traverse the sinking mud and deep stream, my own way. I would replace her lead when we were safely across the other side.

As I picked my way across the firmest of the sodden ground, I saw that Cassie was making much faster and more elegant progress than I, as she bounded lightly over the mud bog and leapt into the water and out again. As she was making much better progress I forgot her for a few seconds, as I carefully considered each perilous footfall. The mud sucked at my boots and then the stream stung with cold on my calves, but determination won the day and I pressed on, wading through the boggy stream and the mud beyond, and I reached the far bank and began to scramble up it. Cassie's lead was still in my hand and as I pulled myself up the bank, holding tussocks of grass here and there, I looked up to see if she had made it safely, my lead at the ready to leash her.

Cassie was already a hundred yards away, in full flight running toward the sheep that I had set out to save!

"Cassie!" I yelled in my loudest voice as I struggled to scramble up the last few feet of the bank. "Cassie, no!" I screamed, horrified.

I got to the top of the bank, clinging to the sides, heaving myself up. I couldn't quite believe that my dog, the one who I thought was terrified of sheep, was now hurtling toward them as fast I as I had ever seen her run. Maybe she had been enthused by the other dog and the fact that the sheep were running? I didn't know why she was suddenly intent on the sheep, but I did know that this was a bad, bad situation, unfolding at very high speed.

"Cassie, no! Cassie, leave it! *Liiieeee down! Stay there!* Cassie, nooooo!" All the commands I had taught her. The things I knew she knew how to do.

Please, no. Please, Cassie, don't do this. Please. I begged her in my mind. Even then, with so much unknown, all I could think was that this situation was *bad*, very, very bad.

Up until this moment Cassie had always been very responsive to all that I had asked of her. She was attentive, watched me and loved me nearly as much as I loved her. But as I reached the top of the bank and began to run as fast as I could toward the sheep, my heavy, mud-covered and water-filled boots weighed me down, and I realised that I had clearly made some terrible mistake in my assessment of her. I dragged myself across the field as quickly as I could, floundering at first due to my weighty boots. When I was barely a quarter of the way across the first field I could see that she had nearly reached the edge. She now faced a stout barbed wire fence on new wooden posts. In impressive style and without breaking her stride she leapt over the fence, clearing it easily, seemingly without any effort, and she began a very athletic climb up the hill toward another fence, this one a line of wire on sticks which I knew to be an electric fence.

For the first time in my dog-owning life I felt totally out of control. Cassie had never failed her recall before in flight. She had been the easiest and most intelligent dog I had ever trained. She *wanted* to please me, of that I was sure. I had taken care to train her to come out of a chase situation with her ball! I'd also taught her to lie down on the way to her ball in full flight and she had always responded. I tried repeatedly to call, to tell her to stop, but as I ran at my fastest speed, my breath was in short supply and I barely managed to shout her name I was so wanting for breath. I felt for the first time totally at a loss as to what to do. So I just kept on running. I both marvelled and despaired at her speed as she bounded up the incline toward the still terrified and fleeing sheep, to join the Lurcher-type dog in his game. She took off again in full flight, clearing the electric fence with ease, and she appeared so confident, her tail mid-height; her utter commitment clear. She was intent in a way I had never seen her before, and she was taking no notice of anything I said. She had never refused to do anything before. She had done all I had asked her to. But now she was doing her thing, 'dog stuff'. Chasing things that run. She had changed from a pet dog into a predator, it seemed.

I was utterly stunned and mortified. I looked from Cassie up the hill, to see a now-awful scene, the sand-coloured Lurcher still running among sheep, taking them down and now, amongst the foray, was my beloved Cassie. She was running alongside the lower edge of what remained of the flock and it looked like she was just having fun. She wasn't running among them like the Lurcher, she was just running alongside them in the same direction. Her tail was now up and she bounded along happily, barking periodically, clearly intent on running with all these animals that were running.

She might even have been following her German Shepherd instincts to herd the fragmenting flock back together, I just didn't know.

She didn't seem to want to grab them or hurt them, just run alongside them. It seemed almost like play. But the sheep didn't know she was playing and the Lurcher looked to me like he was more trying to kill the sheep as he split them off one by one and grabbed them at the back of the neck. A couple of them fell and lay still where they landed, seemingly dead. As I looked further round the field, to my horror I saw that there were increasing numbers of white blobs; apparently dead sheep scattered about the field. Whitish blobs of death by dog lay sombrely amongst the madness, like boulders of granite left out of place by a glacial drift. It looked like a massacre. I felt my heart pounding and my lungs bursting as I renewed my efforts to get there quickly.

Years later I would come to realise that sheep, when exhausted or terrified and unable to get away, can and do drop to the ground and pretend to be dead. Many dogs will pass by a sheep which has collapsed in this way and it is a funny thing to see that minutes later, after the dog has gone, the sheep can get up and seem fine. There are a lot of dogs that will not chase something that isn't running. The predatory chase process – orient, stalk, chase, catch, kill – is thought to be a hardwired mental sequence in the dog, which if interrupted, is halted. So when the sheep stop running the sequence is halted, so the dog won't chase and therefore they are not likely to attack. I find it fascinating that sheep know this, when it took years for mankind and science to figure this out about dogs.

But I didn't know that back then and it seemed to me as if there had been mass murder up there. It filled me with horror. Shaking violently with the shock and now very unsteady on my exhausted legs, I reached the barbed wire fence and placing one hand on top of the fence post, I scissored my legs over the fence in one leap as I had seen my father do once, years ago. Thankfully I cleared it in one leap and I was running again, up the incline now and toward the electric fence. The dogs still ran amongst the sheep and the sheep that were still on their feet kept splitting and running for their lives.

Reaching to the very bottom of my lungs and energy reserves, I speeded my approach as best I could, when suddenly I became aware of more movement above and I could vaguely make out the noise of an engine. I slowed slightly as I took in the scene as a Land Rover sped across the hilltop, toward the gate that would lead to the field with the terrified sheep in it. The field my dog was running amok in.

Oh no, can it get any worse? I thought as I realised that the farmer would arrive at the field before I would and he would see my dog running amongst his sheep. What if he had a gun? What if he shot Cassie? I knew he was within his legal rights to do so and I could imagine his anger at seeing his sheep dotted all over the field, apparently dead.

I realised that I was not going to reach the sheep field quick enough and I slowed to a halt to see what the farmer would do.

The Land Rover came to an abrupt halt and a few seconds later I saw the burly figure of a big man step into the field where the frantic sheep were still running about. From his position high on the hill, he would have been able to see clearly the sheepy mess that lay before him. The 'dead' sheep, the running, diving, grabbing Lurcher at the top of the field and Cassie below on the hill, running alongside his flock dodging the granite-like 'dead' sheep as she ran.

I noted with dread that he was indeed carrying a gun. I couldn't believe just how bad things had got in the space of just a few minutes.

My breath had now failed me as I reached the electric

fence, and realising there was nothing I could do other than shout for him not to shoot, I stood to watch the horror unfold. With what breath I could muster I shouted to the farmer to please not shoot. My lungs were screaming for air and my heart pounding in my chest and as the reality of the situation hit me I felt faint and I swayed on my exhausted legs.

"Noooooooooo! Please don't shoot," I pleaded weakly, with what breath I had left.

Poised at the top of the hill, silhouetted against the heavy, grey, rain-filled sky, I saw him slowly and deliberately raise his gun and take aim. There were a few seconds where he must have been waiting for a clean shot. It seemed like an eternity.

And then several things happened all at once.

The shot rang out around the valley, bouncing back and forth off the valley sides. The sand-coloured dog at the top of the hill fell heavily as if he were a sack of potatoes and lay there like a dead dog. At the moment of the bang, shocked by the sudden noise, Cassie immediately disengaged from the sheep, and her attitude changed from happy, bounding dog 'playing' with sheep, to terrified dog running flat out, tail tucked, down the hill toward me. I looked up at the farmer with his gun and I began to realise that he had turned and now taken aim at my Cassie. Cassie was running straight at me and the farmer was directly in the line of sight behind her from where I stood. Albeit still a long way off, I was looking up the barrel of his shotgun, above the head of my terrified dog. I realised that if he took a shot at her retreating figure, he would also have a chance of shooting me. I didn't mind if he shot me. I felt I deserved it for being so stupid. If my dog was shot then I would prefer to be shot. He must have realised the same thing at the same time, and I saw with the biggest amount of relief that he then lowered his gun and turned away, back toward his Land Rover. Cassie, for this moment at least, was safe. I took a breath, realising that I hadn't been breathing for many seconds.

Cassie was still heading down the hill at breakneck speed, terrified, and as she neared me, she had just the low electric fence to clear and she would be with me. I was so glad she was running to me and not away. But I began to wonder if she was actually planning to stop when she reached me, or just keep running past me. Her eyes were bulging with fear and the headlong gallop down the steep incline was unbalancing her, and I presume this is what made her misjudge the jump over the electric fence. She took off rather unstably on the uneven ground and with an impressive bound she leapt easily high enough to clear the fence, but she had taken off way too far away and she came down on top of it. Her front legs had cleared the lower strand of wire but not the higher one, and the top wire hit her in the chest and she screamed in further terror as she landed and the electric shock jolted through her body. She swung her head round as if to free herself but somehow caught the lower strand on her muzzle, and lifting it up in her flailing attempts to free herself, she looped it over her head. She was now entwined by the two strands and screaming again as the shock ran through her body.

As if things were not already bad enough, I now had to free my girl from the electric fence which entwined her. As I tried to unravel her, she kept screaming and she leapt about in the fence, and I shouted out too as the electricity jolted up my arm and through both our bodies. A few seconds of thought about how I was to free her and I realised I was just going to have to hold the wires one in each hand and pull them apart, taking the shocks as I tried desperately to free her. Simultaneously we jolted and jerked as the electricity pulsated through us time and again.

I twitched and yelled and she screamed as I untangled

her, but thankfully I had soon freed her and I lay on my side, holding her tightly by the collar as she desperately tried to scrabble away from me and keep running, still utterly terrified. In the middle of all the commotion and exhausted now from all that had happened, I looked up weakly from the floor to see the farmer, who had now arrived after what must have been a perilous journey down the steep slope in his vehicle and was striding toward me with intent, the gun cocked over his arm.

He looked as wild-eyed as Cassie had done moments earlier. Direct fear now renewed my energy and I stood quickly, put the lead on Cassie and pulled her behind me in case he still wanted to shoot her. *I must protect my dog from this man with his gun*, I told myself. His face was flushed crimson with anger and his messy and greying hair had bits of straw in it.

I pulled Cassie in close with her lead to the back of my legs, placing myself between my dog and the angry farmer. She was still trying to get away, but I hung on, knowing her only protection from the justifiably angry man was to stay close to my body.

"Is *this your* dog?" he yelled in anger, nodding pointedly at the dog, who was still scrabbling to get away behind me.

"Yes, oh, I'm sorry. So, so sorry!" The words fell out of me in a rush.

"Is *that* your dog?" He gestured with his arm and a roll of his eyes up the hill to where the Lurcher still lay, motionless.

"No, I saw it running in the sheep field, I was walking down there." I pointed to the field below by the stream where my rucksack still lay like an upturned turtle. He followed my pointing arm and gaze with his own. "I was trying to help the sheep."

"Help them?" he fumed. "Are you bloody mad? You thought you would help them by letting your dog run them till they dropped dead?"

"No. No. I'm so sorry. I was trying to stop the other dog."

I pointed once more toward the apparently dead dog at the top of the hill, but further words failed me, emotion took me and I sunk to my knees and began to sob. Pulling the still panicky Cassie close to me, I sobbed into her neck.

The farmer, despite his anger, must have taken some pity on this sobbing female form as his attitude changed a little and he paused before his next, more considered words.

"I was this close to shooting your dog. And you!" I presumed some gesture had accompanied the words 'this close', but my face was still buried in Cassie's fur as relief overwhelmed me that she was still alive. But at the same time I felt sick that the other dog and some sheep were dead.

"I'm so sorry."

"This is private land. How did you get here?" he enquired, seeming calmer.

"I crossed the stream down there. I was walking on the footpath." I looked below us and pointed again to the rucksack that still lay there. "When I saw the dog chasing the sheep, I… I thought, well, errr… I was trying… to help. I didn't know that my dog would… she's never done anything like this before. She is usually, err…" A proper explanation evaded me, but as I looked up at him I could see that his face had softened and was no longer crimson, but just a shade of dark red. He began to realise that my involvement and Cassie's had been well intended but foolishly misguided. I was still clinging to Cassie and she, still trying to get away, had dragged me a short way down the hill. To him it must have been a very humorous sight if it were not for the terrible sight of death up the hill, above us all.

There had been a lack of critical thinking on my part. I hadn't known at the time, but there had also been a lack of adequate knowledge and appropriate prior experience.

After the farmer calmed a bit, I calmed a bit and still holding Cassie close I looked up the hill at the sheep, who were now huddled far away in a corner, still looking wary but no longer running in fear. Steam rose from them as they heaved and panted, trying to recover from their terrifying ordeal, and the running up and down the hill, laden with soon-to-be-born lambs. Surprised, I noticed that most of the blobs of what I thought to be dead sheep had disappeared, and as I watched, the last two remaining 'dead' sheep suddenly got up and ran up the hill, still wary, but apparently unharmed. They made their way back to the relative safety of the panting, steaming flock. They hadn't been dead at all. Just exhausted and terrified. I looked up to where the Lurcher lay, hoping he too might be standing. He, it seemed, had not been so lucky.

It was an awful experience and one that I learned a great deal from. The farmer, once he had calmed, was clearly upset about his sheep and the lambs they were carrying. He even appeared sad about the Lurcher he had killed, but he was pragmatic, the way that many farmers are.

"These things happen," he said. He explained that after such a trauma it was possible that some of his ewes might die, over the next few days, from the shock. He also stated something I already knew: that it was also likely that some of these ewes would miscarry their lambs or give birth at full term to stillborn, or unfit lambs because of the trauma.

After I had apologised as many times as he would allow me, he advised me that he expected me to pay for any dead sheep and lambs that might be aborted following the trauma that had happened, and that if he saw my dog off lead anywhere on his land again then I would be in serious trouble. But I think he realised that I had had good intentions and that this event had been almost as terrifying for me as it had for his sheep.

After taking a long, hard look at my still panting and frightened dog, and a long, hard look at me, with mud up to my knees, all over my clothes and my tear-stained face, he surprised me by offering to give me a lift in his Land Rover, back to my rucksack, taking me round his fields so that I didn't need to go back across the muddy stream.

Loading Cassie into the cab and stepping in behind her, I accepted the offer and we chatted on the way back across the fields, over a little stone bridge back to my rucksack. He told me that only a week earlier the same Lurcher had run amok among one of his other flocks further up the valley. He had taken his gun, and not wanting to shoot the dog – "What person wants to have to shoot somebody's pet dog?" – he said, he had fired a couple of shots into the air, hoping to scare the dog away and save his sheep. Just as Cassie had, the Lurcher had run away, frightened by the gun, and had headed back down the valley toward a nearby village. I noted in my mind from that conversation that the Lurcher had previously run from the gunshot, just as Cassie had today, but he had returned. Very sadly, he had returned. The farmer hoped that the dog would have been sufficiently shocked by the gunshot to avoid involvement with his sheep again, and he had hoped to never see the animal again. He had put posters up in the village shop asking if anyone knew the owner of a sandy-coloured Lurcher dog, and explaining that it had caused the death of two of his pregnant ewes and that he would shoot it if it was seen loose on his land again. No one had come forward to claim responsibility for the dog.

He also explained that he had three public rights of way crossing his beautiful land, and that sadly this also meant that every year, he would lose sheep and/or lambs to dog attacks. Dogs who, just like Cassie, had followed the powerful instincts within them to chase prey animals.

He didn't blame the Lurcher or any of the other dogs who had chased his sheep – they were just dogs being dogs, he said. No, he held the owners responsible for that, and he said wryly that perhaps if the law were to allow him to shoot the owners instead of the dogs, it would be easier to justify his own actions to himself. He had never wanted to shoot anyone's dog, but he didn't want to lose all his sheep either!

Although I knew that dog attacks on sheep did happen, I had no idea that they were so common, or indeed so deadly!

I'm not sure that I would have been as calm and polite as he was, had they been my sheep!

He dropped me in the field by my rucksack and went off in his vehicle back up the fields, toward the Lurcher's lifeless body. Silhouetted again on the hill, I watched him now as he carefully lifted the floppy body of the dead dog and placed it gently in the back of the Land Rover.

I wondered if there would be children at the Lurcher's home missing the dog tonight. Or indeed if it had a home at all prior to this terrible event.

I had agreed to pay for any injured or dead lambs or sheep and a few months later I did get a bill for around £600, for lambs that had been lost, and for three ewes who had been found dead within the next few days in the field. Shock can, and that day, did, kill. When I realised who the letter and bill were from, I cringed inside as I relived the terrible events of that day and I felt sad and sick that so many lives had been lost. That the sheep had been so traumatised that they had aborted their unborn lambs, or that lambs had been stillborn. I paid him without question. I was grateful and thankful to him for sparing the lives of my dog and me that day and I vowed to do all I could to make sure that the events of that day served as educational, somehow. I set out to find out *why* my dog had ignored me and chased the sheep that day. I needed to know more and if I could, somehow, try to reduce the numbers of sheep attacks by dogs.

So why did Cassie, who had previously appeared so scared of sheep, suddenly set off without me, to chase the sheep that day?

Of course it can never be possible for me to know exactly why she did that. When I look back now, the memory I have has no doubt changed somewhat from what actually happened, as is the way of memories. Plus, I can only remember now what I thought I understood and had seen at the time. Had I seen the same thing today, with the vast increase in knowledge, age and experience I have, I might well see something totally differently. In the same way that an experienced police officer can look at a crime scene and notice just the most relevant and important things, dismissing irrelevant aspects, whereas someone new to the role might be unaware as of yet exactly what is and what is not important, and focus because of that inexperience on irrelevant or unimportant factors.

Certainly at that time, the knowledge I had needed to make a more sensible choice about what to do to help the sheep was wholly inadequate. My knowledge of predatory or chase behaviour in dogs was very limited. My knowledge of working sheepdogs and how they come to be trained was completely absent. I had only known in any detail around a dozen dogs. I had 'sort of' trained a working cow dog, but had yet to have any involvement in the training and working of sheepdogs. So I therefore had no real knowledge of how to control a dog safely around sheep without a lead and by using body language, pressure and release, plus vocabulary and commands. I had some, but very limited, knowledge of sheep and how they behaved when in a panic or fearful of a running dog. I also had yet to realise the tremendous impact an owner's motion and movement can have on a dog that shares a bond with its owner. All of these missing bits of information were crucial. And most important, they were crucially absent. And deadly. I certainly would not take the same approach today that I did on that fateful day!

So whilst I cannot ever know for sure, I think it likely that

that terrible day unfolded the way it did because of one of the following reasons, or perhaps a combination of some or all of them!

Firstly, I now realise much more fully that a dog's reaction to a stationary sheep (or bike, car, jogger, rabbit, squirrel, cow, horse, ball, leaf etc.) can be completely different from their reaction to the same thing when it is moving. Indeed, it is common in sheepdog-training circles to use another more experienced dog to get a flock of sheep moving, if a young dog in its early training days is showing reluctance to approach them, as can sometimes happen. Once sheep are moving a different set of instincts is ignited in a dog and they can suddenly begin a chase that they had never even contemplated when the 'thing' was stationary. I definitely believe that by seeing the sheep in full flight, Cassie was primed to become involved somehow.

Secondly, dogs have a truly amazing capacity to read intent. It is my belief that many dogs spend much of their time trying to work out what it is their owner wants of them. The more intelligent the animal, the more this happens. In my experience most dogs *want a job to do*. Indeed, in the absence of being given a job to do, they can sometimes become self-employed! And some of the more intelligent ones, like the herding breeds, become expert at looking to see if they can 'help' in a situation. There are numerous stories of dogs rescuing people that they do not even know, or informing a person when another person is in trouble; of trained guide dogs and hearing dogs seeming to work with their owners and understand their challenges, far beyond the level of their training, seemingly wanting to 'help'. Additionally, many of the farm dogs I've worked with have learnt, without any help from their handlers, how to control the movement of animals around the yard, taking it upon themselves to put young farm animals back into the correct pens, with their mothers, after they have escaped to run riot outside their pens. I also watched in fascination as one of my farming friends' dogs, three Collies and a Rottie cross, jumped into the cattle pens each morning to move the animals first safely away from the gate, so the tractor that was carrying their food was able to enter, and then stand guard as the silage bale was lifted high in the tractor's forks, before being dropped into the feeding ring. The dogs kept the cattle away from the dangers of the tractor and the heavy bale of food. Once the outer cover had been cut away and the bale dropped into the feeding ring, the dogs retreated from the pen, without being called, leaving the animals to feast in peace. They had worked out for themselves, with no training, what was required and how to do it. As new and younger dogs were brought onto the farm they too seemed to quickly join the 'working party', helping their owners and keeping the cattle safe.

Thirdly, that day, as I had observed for the first time what was happening in the field above, Cassie had stood at my side and watched with me as the sheep had begun to career around the field at the top of the hill. She had then been taken by surprise when I had turned so suddenly and sharply, away from the path we had been following for so long at a sedate pace, and had begun to run quickly straight at the sheep that we had both seen, charging around in the field above. She had been invigorated by my change of speed and joined me enthusiastically. Speed arouses dogs. She would no doubt have seen and read my change of attention and attitude from bumbling along in the field without a care, to stopping, looking, turning sharply and beginning to run straight toward the running sheep. Indeed, the actions I took – stop, look, turn, run – formed an almost direct parallel with the known chase behaviour sequence of predators, which is orient, stalk, chase, catch, bite, kill, eat. She could perhaps have perceived my panic and would have heard me shout out "No" to the Lurcher. It would be clear to any person that had seen me from a distance that my intentions had changed at the time the sheep started running, and anyone watching would have been able to see that I was planning on running up that hill directly toward the sheep. It was obvious. Perhaps it was obvious to her? Perhaps she realised that and set off to do what she thought needed doing, or what she thought I thought needed doing? Or perhaps my approach behaviour, so close to that of a predatory animal's inborn instinct, had triggered in her the need to commence hunting. Certainly she had come to read my intentions when we ran together around an agility circuit and she had often read my movements, which determined her course, before running on ahead of me to complete an obstacle that she knew I was aiming her at. Was she simply pre-empting my behaviour and trying to do what she thought I wanted?

Fourthly, now having had experience of training sheepdogs and working with them, I have come to realise that the way Cassie was running around the edge of the sheep, not amongst them, and the way that she tried repeatedly to get to the front of the running melee, is almost reminiscent of a working dog trying to gain control of a flock, gather them together and bring them back to the shepherd. The basic instinct in most working Border Collie sheepdogs is as follows. Imagine a flock of sheep all bunched up together in a rough circle of wool. Imagine that circle from above as a clock face. If I as a shepherd stood more or less level with the six o'clock position on the clock face, then my dog, following its instincts, will automatically stand at twelve o'clock, opposite me, on the other side of the sheep. For this is where the dog can best control the flock and stop them running from me. From the twelve o'clock position, it is also the case that the sheep are likely to move away from the dog and toward me, at six o'clock. If I turned my body and walked round the clock face to, say, nine o'clock, it would be normal for the instincts of a sheepdog, even with no training, to move automatically to three o'clock, to again ensure maximum control of the sheep from the opposite side of the flock. Under normal circumstances a sheepdog will mirror the movements of the shepherd from the other side of the flock. That is *instinct*. It doesn't necessarily need to be trained. Was it possible that Cassie was trying to run around the sheep to the other side to bring them to me? To bring them under control? Was she in fact trying to gather the sheep, not chase them? I could not be sure. The sheep were so panicked and were splitting off in all directions, so Cassie kept changing directions as they did, so I can never know for sure. But it is possible that she was trying to help me, or indeed help the Lurcher?

From the time that I had assessed Cassie's interest in sheep and concluded that she was scared of them, to the sheep-chasing event, Cassie had been continually growing in confidence. Indeed, I had gone out of my way to ensure that this was the case, exposing her to new things, giving her challenges she could succeed at, making her feel safer and cared for. I see it so often in rescue dogs: they start off all coy and wussy and as they grow in confidence they start to do new things. Things that take their owners by surprise. Was it the case that Cassie had simply lost her fear of sheep, albeit temporarily? Personally I think this the least likely reason, but as I can never actually know for sure, I still see it as a possibility and one worthy of consideration for the owners of all dogs. They grow in confidence and they change.

The times I have heard an owner say to me, "He has never done anything like this before" (chased the sheep, bitten a passer-by, raided the bin, stole some food from an owner's plate, pinned another dog to the floor, chased a cat across the road etc., etc.).

My reply to anyone who says, "He has never done anything like this before" is, "None of us, people or dogs, ever did anything like 'that' before, until the day we first did it." I never ate chocolate until the first day I ate chocolate, and I have been eating it ever since. Much to the chagrin of my dentist. It's the same with wine. So now when someone says, "He has never done it before", I point out that now at least they know that from this point forward, he is now more likely to do it again, at least if the thing was enjoyable for the dog. Rewarding activities are repeated when the opportunity arises. Dogs who have bitten, and the bite made a threat go away, are now more likely to bite. Dogs that have a chance to chase sheep, joggers, cars etc. are then more likely to do it again, unless the incident ended badly for the dog.

In Cassie's case she reverted immediately after the sheep-chasing event to being fearful and avoiding sheep. More fearful than she had been before, even. But then her chasing event had ended with being electrocuted on the fence as well as the sound of gunshot and then my tears, so perhaps because of those things, Cassie was now less likely to chase sheep. I don't know; she never got another chance.

These days, with a lot more experience behind me, I often get asked if I can help people to make their dog lose interest in sheep or indeed cars or motorbikes, skateboarders or joggers. I know that with some dogs it is possible to train them to leave sheep and other things well alone even if they are in motion. I know it because I have trained a couple of my own dogs very successfully to do just that. Lace, Mirk and Connor were all trained in such a way that they would leave well alone sheep or other running animals, or moving things (as in cars). However,

Cloud *could not be trained against such things*. She was retired from sheep work for a variety of reasons, but one of them was that even when the sheep were penned, or grazing far away, she would still feel the need to pester them or make them run. I couldn't stop her from doing it, such was her intent, and even my sheepdog instructor, a world-famous handler of enormous skill, couldn't stop her either. So for Cloud, there was no other option than life on a lead wherever stock might be present. Karma, my most recent dog, will never be trusted off lead with sheep either. Or anything else, because she operates via a completely different and to me mysterious set of instincts altogether, due to her diagnosed 'learning difficulties'.

All the dogs I trained to cease sheep-bothering on command were all trained, working sheep or cow dogs to some degree. But even with those dogs, unless they were my sheep or sheep belonging to someone who knew I was using them, I would still keep my dogs on leads around unfamiliar stock, because the sheep don't know how well behaved the dog is. Nor does the sheep's owner, and more importantly, what if my dog's formerly 'sheep-proof' status was changed and it suddenly did something it had never done before, just as every other dog and person in the world can do?

So when people ask me for my help to keep their dog safe against the risks of them chasing sheep or other things, I say that the best thing to do is to keep the dog on a lead, or keep it away from stock altogether. That in my view is the *only* way to know for sure that your dog is safe in all situations. Whenever it is safe to do so, my dogs are run free off lead. But if it isn't safe, I think back and remember looking up the barrel of that farmer's gun and I reach for my leads to protect my dogs and myself.

Please be aware that in the UK, the Countryside Code states that your dog must be kept on a lead where livestock are grazing, and that if the owner of stock considers that your dog is or has been bothering their stock then by law they have the right to shoot to kill your dog.

I have since seen the sheep-chasing story from both sides of the coin, after a loose GSD twice ran amongst sheep that I personally was responsible for, the first time causing some injuries and one death. The second time, there were six dead ewes, all of them in lamb. Three of them died long, agonising and painful deaths, as we were unable to get to them for several hours. Some of the details of the terrible deaths are too traumatic for me to write here. Others seemingly died quite quickly. There were over a dozen unborn lambs lost from live ewes and the whole flock repeatedly miscarried for several years after the terrible attacks. Even though they were moved to another field the very next day, they never truly recovered and they always suffered trauma-related problems. They never flourished again. To them, the world was a potentially very scary place and they never seemed peaceful having seen so many of their sheep mates being killed in such terrifying circumstances.

Please keep your dogs safe. Keep farm animals safe and keep everyone happy. Keep your dog on a lead around livestock. Then you, or your dog, may never face the barrel of a gun.

And to my beloved Cassie, I must offer deep gratitude for teaching me as she did and for helping me understand what it was that I didn't, and still don't, completely understand: what it is to be a dog.

You were my best friend and one of my greatest lessons. Run free, lass, and avoid the sheep, my treasured friend.

Over the Moon!

When the call came in, the owner reported that Moon, a young female Staffie, had been involved in several fights. Though she was thought to have caused them, it was only Moon that got hurt, though nothing more serious than a sore ear or minor graze. On the phone I couldn't quite get to the bottom of *how* Moon was thought to be causing the fights, so we had her brought in for an assessment.

Moon was an eighteen-month-old neutered female. On lead she was friendly with all dogs, I was told, and she played often with the owner's other dog. But early in her life she had got involved in several noisy scuffles and since about six months old she had been kept on lead away from other dogs. Her owner, worried about the reputation that Staffies have for fighting with dogs, had seen the scuffles as more serious than they sounded, and wanting to avoid serious injury, had chosen to play it safe and kept her on lead.

Recently though her owner had wanted to acquaint her with a friend's dog, so she had decided to seek help with the problem. I queried how it was that Moon was causing the fights and the owner replied with things like: "The other dogs just don't like her"; "She hasn't got the best manners"; "She doesn't approach right"; "She is a bit too boisterous/too rude." Her owner seemed somehow embarrassed and coy, so I dug for more information. But every question I asked led to the same spurious 'work-around' answers: "She just doesn't behave properly", "It's not appropriate"; and the owner grew visibly more embarrassed with each attempt she made to explain.

Eventually I asked the owner to describe what she had seen the last time there was an off-lead encounter with a strange dog. I was told that Moon had just rushed straight up to a dog and "jumped on it". The dog had almost immediately set about Moon and there had been some terrible noises, and they had been grappling for several seconds before being separated. I dug deeper. The noise was terrible, the owner had said, and it made her feel so sick inside.

"What do you mean," I interjected, "by 'jumped on it'?"

She hung her head in shame; by now she was sweating and her cheeks glowed red. She replied, "Just, you know, jumped on it."

Getting to the root cause of an owner's request for help is often harder than one might think it ought to be. Sometimes they feel that the dog trainer is going to judge them. They might already have been judged or belittled by another trainer or by someone on the internet. The internet can be a hateful and hurtful place, I know that myself! Sometimes their life experience has made them expect that of people. I explained that anything she said was unlikely to surprise me, and that I was on her side. I was not going to judge her or tell her she was wrong. I was quite sure that whatever was happening and whatever involvement she had, she had tried her best and meant well. I explained I was willing and wanting to help them both.

In this case though it was embarrassment at her dog's behaviour that was the fence between my questions and her answers. She didn't want to tell me what the dog was doing, because to her it was too shocking and rude.

Her clear embarrassment was the indicator that I needed to ask the question that I had asked many times before of embarrassed owners: "Do you mean jumped on it in a *humping* kind of way? As in having sex with it?"

Her head bowed. "Yes, yes, in that way," she replied, avoiding eye contact, shame evident, but clearly relieved that someone had finally 'said it'. Poor lady. I see this so often: people reluctant to talk about what they see as sexual acts, or which *are* sexual acts, or something they see as dog 'perversions' or antisocial 'sexually abnormal' behaviour.

I've worked on various farms throughout my life and in the process learnt plenty about and seen often the various reproductive acts and processes of animals, and having discussed these important activities openly and liberally with farming friends, it always seems odd to me when people become so embarrassed or ashamed when discussing them. But it is so very common amongst dog owners. Over the years I had discussed at length, and often with humour, the bull who 'couldn't reach his target', rams that were 'firing blanks' (producing infertile semen), a bull whose testicles had been bitten by an adder and swelled to the size of footballs (not at all funny, the bull had to be put to sleep), and supposedly breeding animals who simply lacked libido.

On top of that, during five years of schooling, on many sunny days there were two male dogs that spent a lot of time humping on our school premises, in a place that many of us could see from our classrooms. At first we all thought it was funny but eventually it just became normal for us.

I feel so sorry for some owners. Moon's poor owner was squirming and sweating and looking so embarrassed the whole time. I find it so sad that some people find discussion and the sight of normal animal behaviour so excruciatingly difficult and painful, when all they have is a dog, being a dog.

Whilst humping other adult dogs is not ideal (unless it's an intentional mating), it isn't uncommon and is usually pretty easily resolved.

So having established that Moon had 'jumped on' several dogs, both male and female, who had told her off and got into scuffles for it, we decided to see how she behaved with a stooge. At that time I had Cloud. Now Cloud was an extraordinary dog who could read other dogs' behaviour in a way I have never seen any other dog do. We had come to rely on her response to any dog as a clear assessment of whether there was any ill intent there. She had never failed to get it right. After this event, she and I once failed together, but that is a later story!

As well as splitting fights, halting aggressive onslaughts, teaching manners and being able to assess a dog's behaviour in some unidentifiable way, she could also spot and 'nanny' weak or nervy dogs. What was sure was that if there was ill intent in Moon, then Cloud would let me know. So on lead, at a distance of five metres, we introduced Moon to Cloud. Cloud's reaction was clear – utter disinterest. We brought her closer, and Moon was very excited, wagging her tail like mad and giving off all sorts of clearly visible, friendly play signals. Cloud was unimpressed and just went about the business of disregarding the client dog and eating liver cake. I asked if the excitement shown by Moon was normal for her. It was. It was beginning to look to me like Moon was very friendly but had a habit of humping other dogs that got her some severe tellings-off, which it appeared Moon had never understood. So, convinced that Cloud would have recognised any bad intent, we decided to let Moon loose on a bigger dog than her, who was known to be friendly, to see what all the trouble was about.

A large GSD cross was chosen; we'll call him Jim. Big

enough to squish Moon if Moon got out of control, but very friendly and biddable with all dogs. A highly sophisticated communicator, this old boy knew what he was there to do. He loved this work. He strolled around the paddock happily, waiting for the new dog to arrive. We let Moon loose, dragging her lead so that we could easily remove her if necessary, and she flew over to him in a whirling dash of excitement and friendliness. As soon as she arrived, she wriggled and wagged madly at him, unnecessarily aroused, then leapt onto his back as best as she could, and began humping actions immediately. Her owner was staring, embarrassed, at the floor.

"See, she's a pervert!" she said, disgust written all over her face. I pulled Moon gently by her lead off of Jim, who was totally nonplussed, and took her out of the paddock to have a little chat. Moon sure was a happy little thing – she came with me easily, wagging her enthusiastic tail the whole time. Just happy to be alive, it seemed. Her coat shone even though it was light in colour. She smiled that Staffie smile up at me. She really was a sweetie.

Many puppies will hump each other from very early on. Often as they mature the behaviour fades away, but sometimes it remains and will only be quashed if an owner stops it, or if they encounter another dog that successfully communicates that this behaviour is no longer acceptable as adolescent or adult behaviour. With some dogs and bitches, humping can be a stress release when a dog gets over-excited or worried, and it is often considered a displacement activity. A displacement activity is where a dog is confused about what to do.

Imagine this. You're young, unattached and in a cafe. An unknown gorgeous person, of the sex you are attracted to, comes up and says very directly to you, "Wow, I am sure it was you I dreamt of last night. Can I buy you a drink?" They gesture towards a sofa over to one side of the room, wanting to you to go and sit with them. One part of you is immediately attracted to their big smile and pleasing features and is happy to go with them into the sunset, but on the other hand you have in your mind, *Weirdo. What a creepy thing to say. I need to stay away from you*. You are torn. So you don't go with them and you don't walk away from them; instead you bite your lip, or scratch the back of one hand with the other. Those are displacement activities.

It Is also important to note that female dogs, as well as male dogs, sometimes perform humping activities on bitches that are in season, as well as if they themselves are in season, or due in season. That is, if a bitch is in season, other bitches may try to hump it and the bitch in season might try to hump other bitches. This is normal dog behaviour around the time of an animals' season, or 'heat', and is very common and will usually fade away after the season has finished. This is a behaviour common to many species of animals, not just canines. It's normal.

Because the humping had resulted in a few scuffles which had deeply upset Moon's owner she had been put permanently on a lead, meaning that it was no longer possible for another dog to tell Moon off and rectify the situation. The dogs that had got 'cross' with Moon had clearly been unable to get their point across in the little time they had, as immediately that they shouted at Moon, her owner had removed her and the lesson had never come to fruition.

So we took Moon out of the situation and chatted.

Realising that Moon's owner was so embarrassed about what she perceived as her dogs most 'unnatural' behaviour, I explained gently that actually non-functional humping, by both dogs and bitches, to both dogs and bitches, is pretty common. And it doesn't mean that they are sexual predators or abnormal in any way. It's just fairly normal dog behaviour that hasn't been halted by another dog or by the owner. She looked a little relieved.

Further enquiry revealed that there was another dog at home, an older dog who had been there before Moon had arrived as a puppy. There is no doubt that the oldest dog in the household is a crucial and sometimes the primary or only 'dog role model' for any youngster. If a puppy is lucky, the older dog will offer a mixture of support in times when a pup is fearful of something, teach normal play moves to the pup and will also administer 'telling off' when the puppy oversteps the mark or behaves in a way that will not be acceptable to the wider dog population. A bit like a responsible older human brother teaching his little brother that throwing bricks at him hurts and will get him into trouble, so that he doesn't throw bricks at the next-door neighbour's little girl.

Just as children do with adult humans, puppies get leeway from most older dogs in terms of overly boisterous or exuberant play behaviour. Where a puppy is coming into adolescence some puppy behaviours that might have been accepted by other dogs will cease to be acceptable. And it is the job of an older dog, or in the absence of such a dog, the humans, to teach these types of lessons.

It's the same with people. If a two-year-old picks up a felt tip pen and starts to draw on your living room wall, then though it might be irritating, one couldn't really be cross as the child perhaps doesn't know any different.

However, if a fourteen-year-old, or a forty-year-old takes a pen and draws on your wall then chances are you will get cross. Behaviour that is acceptable as a child is not acceptable as an adolescent or grown-up. It's the same with dogs. Whilst humping behaviour in a very young puppy might be somewhat tolerated without reprimand by an adult dog, that same behaviour will often become unwelcomed by most dogs as the pup grows up and will certainly not usually be tolerated by many dogs by the time the pup reaches adolescence.

In many cases, most socially unacceptable behaviours will be ceased by an older, wiser dog either in the home or elsewhere. If the older dog at home tolerates behaviour from a pup that will not be tolerated by other dogs, then the pup has missed out on a very valuable lesson. A lesson that in Moon's case had led her into squabbles with other dogs out on walks. It was the unhelpful tolerance of the older dog at home that had caused Moon's downfall. Moon was regularly and repeatedly humping the older dog at home. The older dog simply lay down and did nothing to tell her off. Poor role models reap poor behaviour toward other dogs.

Telling a dog off is a standard behaviour within dog groups. Growling, snarling, chasing, nipping, air-snapping, freezing, blocking, knocking over, standing over, muzzle-gripping, ear-holding and pinning to the ground, even squishing flat, are all methods that dogs use to 'tell another dog off', or cease an unwanted or undesirable behaviour. These are important and crucial lessons in social skills for any young dog. Sometimes an owner sees what is happening and will stop the older or wiser dog providing these tellings-off, and in those cases the unwanted behaviour goes unpunished and continues. If an older dog is not strong enough or willing to tell off a puppy, then the puppy behaviour is allowed to continue until either another dog or the owner halts the behaviour.

I asked her whether she had tried anything to stop the behaviour herself.

She replied that she had immediately gone and got hold of Moon, put her on a lead and dragged her away. Hugely embarrassed, she had apologised to the other dog's owner.

"What with the reputation of Staffies and that," she said, "I thought it best to keep her away from dogs in case she was being vicious."

So then came the crucial question that to me seems so

obvious, but which I have to ask so often these days: "Have you ever told her not to do it?

She stared at me blankly, without any discernible expression for a few moments, and then repeated the question back to me. "Told her not to do it?"

"Yes," I repeated. "Have you ever told her not to do it?"

"Errrrrr…" Confusion wafted briefly across her face and she repeated the words again, as if trying to taste them, understand them, as if they were being spoken in a foreign tongue. "Told her not to do it…" she said again. This time it wasn't stated as a question, she was merely saying the words and considering them.

I paused whilst she pondered the words more fully.

And then, almost as if she was surprising herself with this sudden realisation, she said, "No. I haven't."

"Well, shall we try that then?" I said, and I took her indoors to give her a brief lesson in telling a dog not to do it.

Away from Moon and the other dogs I taught Moon's owner how to use 'splitting', an act seen commonly in groups of dogs. Many people will have witnessed their dogs 'splitting' other dogs. Many dogs do it routinely and though people do not always understand what they are seeing, when they do, they often marvel at how clever it is. Cloud was an expert splitter. She would use splitting to separate dogs that were humping, fighting (or considering fighting), or animals that were playing over-exuberantly.

A form of splitting is often used by bouncers in nightclubs to halt aggressive interactions. The bouncer will step between the sparring pair, singling out and turning toward the most aggressive, using their body, or sometimes just their arm, to separate them and form a barrier. When humans wish to split dogs, it is best done from some distance, avoiding actual contact.

So with the help of a stuffed toy and a chair to demonstrate, placing the chair over the back of the stuffed toy, as if the chair were humping the toy, I showed Moon's owner how to 'split' two dogs, with body language.

It's usually fairly easy to do. Imagine there are an apple and an orange sat side by side on a table in front of you. The apple is on the right as you view it. If you wish to 'split' the apple and orange, removing the apple from the situation (the apple being Moon), then put your left hand in front of you and with your palm and your body facing the apple, bring your hand down between the two and then quickly flick your hand to toss the apple to one side, away from the orange. That is splitting with contact. When splitting dogs, not pieces of fruit, it's best to make no contact: dogs can often just read the intention. The process is the same except that you do it from several feet or metres away. In your mind you imagine that your hand is extended with an invisible extension, but you still do the same action. Turn your body to face the animal you wish to remove, put your nearest hand to the animal out and pretend to 'slice' between them and then flick your wrist as if tossing the dog to one side.

If it were the orange that you wished to remove (or a dog on the left of the situation), then you would turn your body the opposite way, to face the orange, and use your right hand to 'slice' between the gap, still at a distance of several feet.

We practised with the stuffed toy and the chair until Moon's owner understood the movement perfectly and could do it automatically and with ease.

And then I asked her to do the same thing but at speed and with utter conviction, whilst saying the words: *"No! Stop that right now!"*

At first Moon's owner thought I was bonkers, but I told her I would demonstrate on the dogs and she seemed comforted.

Back into the paddock we went and Jim was once more let loose. Then Moon was released. Full of enthusiasm she repeated the same behaviour as before. With a brief excited whizz around Jim, she bounced onto his back. With her owner at my side I stepped dramatically toward the two dogs, and with my hand extended and with the splitting action of my arm, I shouted, "No! Stop that at once!"

Moon, shocked, got off Jim's back immediately and looked at me, slightly confused. Slightly wary. This had never happened to her before. After a few seconds she recovered and made advances toward the unfazed Jim again. I stepped in again, arm outstretched, performing the split before it was necessary and Moon stopped again. Her crazy enthusiasm had waned slightly and she looked at me dubiously.

"Good girl!" I praised her. She wagged her tail, and disengaging from Jim she ran off to sniff the grass and have a roll. I turned to Moon's owner and she smiled. I could see she was impressed and surprised at how easy it had been to halt Moon's behaviour.

Time for another dog. We brought old Mirk in. Mirk was as laid-back as they come and never aggressive. Old, but still stable and strong, he took everything in his stride. He seemed to enjoy his work with other dogs. With Moon's owner prepared and me at her side in case she needed a shove at the right time, we let Moon into the paddock to face Mirk.

Moon was once again overjoyed, and wagging furiously she ran straight at Mirk, and just as she was about to leap on him, I prodded Moon's owner and said, "Now", and she sprang into action.

With the actions of a pro she stepped assertively toward Moon, her body facing her own dog, her arm outstretched, and shouted, "No! Stop that right now!", just as I had taught her. Excellent. Moon looked stunned and backed away from

Mirk and from her owner. Her tail lowered and she stooped slightly, in a rather surprised display of half-submission. She wasn't frightened, but she was very surprised and she was acknowledging her owner's new behaviour.

"Good girl." Moon's owner, smiling and looking pleased with herself, praised her. Moon stood upright, looked at her owner, wagged her tail, then looked at Mirk, wagged her tail again and trotted off. Mirk trotted off after her, wagging his tail. He didn't understand what had just happened but he liked this little dog and wanted to make friends. Moon, realising she was being followed, stopped and turned to face Mirk. He slowed and wagged his tail. They sniffed and normal dog interactions began.

Moon, realising she couldn't hump Mirk, had to learn some new ways to communicate. But she was already calmed. The split and stern words had made her stop and think, instead of just repeating her normal behaviour. She knew what 'no' meant; she had learnt it as a tiny puppy. She knew the move her owner made toward her was asking her to get away from Mirk. Body language often comes more easily to dogs than to humans!

After a few minutes we released a number of dogs into the paddock and Moon, rather cautiously at first, met each one in a friendly manner and after a few minutes a normal, healthy game of chase had commenced between Moon and one of the young Labradors.

Moon's owner was beaming. "I can't believe it," she said.

It took just three attempts at splitting Moon and being stern and Moon ceased the behaviour. She was a sensitive soul. Not to dogs – she wasn't sensitive to dogs. In her former overly excited approach she hadn't taken time to read or understand them, but humans she did understand. She understood that her owner was unhappy with her when she tried to hump

Mirk and she understood and accepted the reprimand in good faith.

The speed at which we reformed Moon of her humping took me a little by surprise. Every case is different. But in the space of just a few minutes Moon had gone from habitually humping everything on four legs, immediately on sight, to refraining from the habit and learning new ways to relate to dogs. Ways that wouldn't get her ear bitten or start scuffles, and which would allow her to be let safely off lead again. Moon's owner was sent home to meet up with a few dogs owned by friends and to use the same technique if the humping began again.

Moon's owner reported back a week later that Moon had tried once to hump a friend's dog and that she was successful in stopping it immediately. After that Moon had not tried it again. Her owner had also managed to stop Moon from humping the older dog at home, using the same techniques. It was important that the source of all the trouble, the overly patient dog at home, the poor role model, was also protected against Moon's over-vigorous behaviour. Moon's owner reported that the older dog seemed happier now and didn't spend so much time lying in her bed. Moon was now running freely off lead, to mix and mingle happily with other dogs. Now that Moon was not fixated on humping, she seemed to prefer racing games and she had lost weight already with all the new activity. And curiously, for reasons I do not understand, the owner seemed able now to talk about Moon's 'perverted habit' without embarrassment.

It was one of those cases where everyone was happy. Owner, dog, dog housemate, local dogs, friends' dogs and me too! Happy days.

The Commonest Dog Behaviour Problem in the UK

The commonest dog behaviour problem in the UK has the simplest of solutions!

If only we could all see it.

This is not the tale of a particular dog with a problem. This is more the tale of an increasingly growing problem that affects a big percentage of some breeds, or more specifically, crossbreeds. These are many dogs, with lots of problems, which may stem from a single cause. A completely avoidable cause.

Over the many years that I have been involved with dog training and behaviour, the types of problems we see most often fluctuate with the popularity of different breeds. Breeds have breed issues – breed-specific behaviours and training problems; health and maintenance problems that are often specific to the breed.

At the time of writing, the most popular 'breeds' to come through our classes at puppy level are the Cockerpoo (Cocker Spaniel cross Poodle), Labradoodle (Labrador cross Poodle), ShihTzipoo (Shih Tzu cross Poodle), HavaShihTzipoo (seriously, that is the breed name given on our registration form – Havanese cross Shih Tzu cross Poodle), and all the '–poo' or '–oodle' crosses. The problem has always been there in other unusually long, wiry, non-shedding, wavy, or 'scruffy' coats. But it has become so common that these breeds now account for more 'odd' behaviours than any other breeds in our classes. But many of these odd behaviours can be stopped very easily indeed.

The behaviours that these breeds suffer from, sometimes even from a very young age, are, in my experience, as follows:

- A fixation with the floor.
- Chasing shadows.
- Often having the head facing down.
- Changing direction very erratically.
- Holding the head stiffly or at odd angles.
- Turning their heads suddenly and sharply without warning.
- Suddenly jumping and turning 90 degrees in one direction or the other, or turning completely through 180 degrees.
- Snapping at owners' or others' hands as they approach the dog's face, or when they touch the dog's body.
- Sudden jerky movements, then bouts of extreme stillness, or long pauses.
- Being erratic and frantic.
- Running away from things that the owner cannot see or hear.
- Hiding for no apparent reason.
- Not really 'connecting' with the owner.
- Being scatty and scampering a lot.
- Whizzing around without cause.
- A reluctance to be held by unfamiliar people.
- Over-excitement or surprise when held by unfamiliar people.
- Being overly shocked by loud noises; being very scared, freezing and being very still when there are loud noises; cowering, shaking, refusing to move.

- Jumping up at people as if desperate to be lifted up.
- Panic.
- Turning their heads sharply and hitting something – a cupboard door, a door, your knee, maybe, or other people's legs or knees.
- Running into things.
- Bumping into things that are new in their home environment.
- Seeming reluctant to enjoy new experiences.
- Being unusually quiet for a puppy.
- Being unusually manic for a puppy.
- Seeming 'odder' in some indiscernible way than other dogs you have known, but you can't quite describe or understand why.
- Sometimes failing to respond to previously taught behaviour commands, or seeming reluctant to learn, stubborn, or they don't ever make eye contact with their owner, or anyone.
- Continuous fidgeting.
- Being overly still.
- Seeming to 'live in their own world', in a peculiar way that again you can't quite put your finger on.
- Or any number of other behavioural oddities that I haven't listed…

If your dog is an '–oodle' or a '–poo' of any type, or is any other long, scruffy, heavy, wavy, flaxen, wiry or curly-coated breed, and suffers from any of the above, *it might be that your dog can't see very well, because its hair is in the way of its vision*. This is if the hair is over your dog's eyes, around the sides of its face, along the top and sides of its muzzle, or curves around and across the eyes in some way; or if your dog's eyelashes are incredibly long and fast-growing. We have a dog in class at the moment whose eyelashes (not just eyebrows and head hair), have to be trimmed every three weeks, because unless they are, his range of vision is severely impaired and his behaviour becomes odd. If your dog is showing any of the above symptoms then check to see if your dog's vision is being impaired by its hair growth.

Of course there can be many reasons behind the behaviours listed above; it may not just be an issue of hair growth, but it is easy to test for yourself what your dog can and cannot see:

1. Sit in front of your dog in good light and look into his eyes. How much of the eye can you actually see clearly, without looking through any hair? If you can't see part or all of your dog's eyes because of hair, then notice how much of your dog's eye you can actually see. If you can see, let's say, 50% or 10% of their eyes, then the chances are that they can only see the same percentage of you or the world they live in. If you stand close to them, then their ability to see you will be very limited indeed!

2. Let's say you decide you can only see 20% of your dog's eyes. Put your fingers over your own eyes and cover them so that you can only see 20% of what you can normally see. How clear is the world to you now?

3. Still with your fingers obscuring your own vision, now close the curtains, dim the lights or turn them off. How clear is the world to you now?

All sorts of odd behaviours occur when a dog's vision is obscured by hair. Dogs with little hair cover but huge eyebrows, for instance, find it very hard to look up high enough to make eye contact with their owners and are thus often described as 'aloof', when actually they just can't see anyone over their height.

Dogs who have large 'beards' can find it difficult to see

where their own front feet and legs are and can show reluctance to climb into cars, or do agility tasks, or may be ungainly or lack elegance in their front leg movements.

If the visual impairment is left long enough then some puppies and dogs will grow up and behave as a blind dog would. Their brains fail to develop visual acuity as a normal dog with full vision would. And *as the dog starts to rely more and more on sound, their sensitivity to it often becomes extreme*, so that they may react to sounds that no one else can hear, making them erratic and unpredictable in their behaviour.

They don't get enough information into their brains to work out what's going on in the world. A dropped spoon, for instance, can be really shocking to a puppy that heard it hit the floor, but didn't see it drop. When you can't see well, the sounds that you hear can cause confusion and fear. Such dogs can overreact to sound, seem 'mad' or go 'weird'.

All of this can be stopped easily with a good haircut. Or the hair can be tied back with a hair bobble or greased back with non-toxic wax.

I have been advised by groomers (and I am not a groomer so I can only go on their word), that to be sure a dog has full visual potential they need their facial hair tended to about every three to four weeks if their hair is the type to obscure their vision. I hope I have made a case for groomers to help clients understand the need for this regular grooming and care of facial hair in affected breeds. And please, breeders, tell your puppy buyers to ensure the puppy's line of sight is kept clear at all times. Trainers, keep an eye out. Friends, share this wisdom.

Many people can keep their pet's facial hair under control themselves. Please use blunt-ended scissors, and if you are in any doubt about the process, please consult a groomer that has been recommended to you. Just like any profession there are great groomers out there who will care for your pet and treat it kindly, and there are terrible ones that will not treat your dog kindly. Make sure yours is the best that you can find!

Now that is all great and can help many…

But that's not the best bit!

Often when an owner has grown used to not being able to see their dog's eyes, they have failed to realise how much they miss out on.

Looking into a dog's eyes and seeing what lies behind these intelligent, capable, sociable, communicative, mystical, magical, beautiful, amazing animals can be an incredibly powerful, relationship-building process, and is surely what every owner wants.

Your dog *is* what lies behind its eyes. Its personality and mind are in those eyes.

When suddenly a dog's eyes connect once again with its owners' after an absence caused by hair, it is often wonderful to see.

Occasionally if we have an experienced groomer around we will cut a puppy's hair during class time when we notice there is an issue. The effects are instant and dramatic. The puppy just sits there and looks about. If he could speak I'm sure he would be speechless for a few moments. They just stare in a kind of still, calm wonder, as they take everything in. Suddenly they can see again! It's great.

Beware, though – very occasionally, when the hair is cut the puppy or dog might become worried or a bit fearful for a short while. But this will pass in time, and overall, in *every single* case that I have come across to date, everyone benefits from the dog's hair, eyelashes and head hair being brought and kept under control.

Let there be light!

Sabre

As is often the case, sometimes something just 'happens' that at the time seems normal or unimportant, or may even have been an accident or mistake, but which turns out to be a turning point in a life which brings about major changes in the way we view or do things, to such an extent that could never have been predicted when the original incident happened.

This is the story of one such event and a dog called Sabre and his owner, Linda. The story began a long time ago, before Sabre was even born, with a dog called Ben, way back in 1977 when I was around ten years old.

It was an ordinary day and I was doing a very ordinary thing: I was out walking with my friend's Border Collie, a breed I had come to love and admire. At that time I had seen Border Collies working sheep just a few times, but on each occasion I was utterly mesmerised, and I would try to understand how it worked. Something about Collies when they are working sheep hit a very deep chord inside me. I didn't know what exactly happened in me when I saw a dog working sheep, I still don't, but I know it happens to some other people too. It's like magic, like raw nature in a domestic world, and it holds a beauty that to this day still lives in me. I saw the owners, handlers and trainers of such dogs as heroes, as magicians and as people far wiser then I might ever be. Knowing and working sheepdogs was one of those things I longed for, but didn't know if I could ever achieve that ambition.

It was a sunny day and I was walking with Ben along a very little-used country lane, with green hedges either side, no verge and only wide enough for one vehicle. As Ben and I strolled along, listening to the skylarks and the baaing of sheep in fields, enjoying the warmth of the day, I noticed a change in Ben's attitude from relaxed to alert, as he raised his head and sniffed the air, and then his ears tensed, his trotting slowed. Then I heard a commotion. I quickly recognised the sound to be that of hundreds of little hooves, travelling at speed down the lane toward us. They appeared, trotting with intent, a few dozen fluffy white faces. Had they escaped from somewhere? Then came the sound of whistling and I realised that these sheep were probably being followed by a sheepdog and its handler, being driven this way, right toward Ben and me. A sheepdog was coming our way! Hurrah. My senses tingled with anticipation and I marvelled briefly at just how good life was and how lucky I was to be there at that moment.

But my pleasure was short-lived. Almost as soon as the sheep had come into sight, there was a tremendous jolt and a sharp pain in my shoulder as Ben leapt forward in an almighty bound and began a frantic barking, lunging and pulling, trying to drag me toward the oncoming sheep. The lead sheep, startled by the noise and activity that Ben was displaying, halted in their tracks and the rest bunched from behind. I had visions of the sheep turning and running away from Ben and I realised quickly that I had to get him out of the way and cease his commotion for the sheep to feel safe enough to pass us.

Though I was an active country girl and strong for my age, Ben had taken me by surprise and nearly pulled me off my feet, and for a few moments all I could do was to flounder and grapple with him, before regaining my balance. Luckily for me, Ben was a slightly built dog, small for his breed and sex. So with everything I could muster, I leant back on the lead, dug my feet in as best I could and regained my balance and some composure, as my mind searched frantically for a way to stop Ben's leaping and barking.

I had never had a dog I was walking do this before. I had never even seen a dog do this before and I had no idea how to react. Little did I know that in years to come leaping, barking dogs would be a very frequent experience in my everyday life.

I looked round quickly for somewhere to remove Ben to, so that the sheep might pass. With all the strength I had as a young girl, I dragged Ben, still leaping and barking as he was, back up the lane twenty yards and into a gateway we had passed a few moments before. There was no gate so I was able to get him well off the lane and into the entrance to the field that lay beyond.

Still barking and leaping, it seemed to me that Ben had gone completely crazy! I needed to calm and quieten him – quickly. So I did the only thing I could think of. I figured he might be calmer if he couldn't see the sheep.

I remembered that I had once rescued a blackbird from a net: he had flailed his only free wing and had pecked my hand and squawked and wriggled as I'd tried to free him, but I had covered his eyes and then when I'd freed him I had put my hands around him, holding him close to me, firmly but with respect for his frail body. He had stilled once he realised I wasn't letting go and I wasn't going to hurt him either. After calming the bird, a quick check revealed he looked well, and both wings pulled out normally, so although stressed, he seemed unharmed. Hoping he could still fly, I had released the bird moments later and he flew off unharmed. But I had learned a good lesson about how to handle manic, frightened, aggressive or panicky animals, and I began to handle my new chickens at home that way too.

Summoning all my remaining strength and pulling Ben as close as I could with his lead, I reached forward to grab his old leather collar. I caught the crazed animal mid-leap and pulled him in toward me. As I managed to turn his head toward me, I stepped back, pulling Ben away from the lane with one hand. Then I reached out with the other hand and took the other side of his collar to use my wrists to try to still his head. Gently but firmly, I pulled him in close to me with his head facing away from the lane, where in moments I hoped to see the sheep, and the anticipated sheepdog, pass by.

Ben, surprised by my actions, stopped his barking at once and refocused his attention onto me. I'd pulled him close to my thighs and for a moment he pulled back on his collar, fighting me, but realising I was determined to hold on, he relaxed a little and I felt him calm slightly, and then he gave up the fight. As Ben was quiet now, still holding him, I glanced up quickly, hoping to see the sheep, and as I did so, Ben sensed my lack of attention and catching me by surprise again, whirled around. Unbalancing me, he freed himself from my grip and immediately once again commenced his barking and leaping. But I still had the lead, so once more I pulled him in close and taking his collar, turned him toward me and held him close to my body, his bum once more facing the anticipated sheep. His face close to my thighs, he could still hear the sheep but not see them. Again his barking ceased and this time, he seemed to calm almost instantly.

The sheep began to file past the gateway as I held onto Ben, averting his gaze from the flock as they continued their passage down the lane. As I looked up to see if the sheepdog was coming yet, I felt Ben give up his attempts to pull back against me, and sensing he had calmed, I released his collar but kept hold of his lead. He turned once more to the sheep, but this time he just uttered a few little woofs. As soon as he woofed, I once again took his collar and stepping back, I pulled him close once more to me. I had to stop him barking. This time, he moved toward me easily, understanding my intent, and he stood facing me, compliant and biddable. He seemed to have forgotten the sheep. I released his collar and he turned back to the sheep but made no attempt to bark or lunge. He stood, calmly and loosely watching, as I did, as the sheep and finally the dog trotted past. He seemed genuinely curious as to what they were doing, but the mania of a few moments before was completely gone.

And there, in a few frantic moments of grappling with Ben, was born the very early beginnings of a technique that was to bring me great success in resolving on-lead dog-to-dog reactivity cases. A technique that was to be developed and refined and used in dozens of cases in the future. The technique that would bring me success, bring moments of wonder, reduce owners to tears of joy, get me into terrible heated arguments with those that didn't believe me, get me thrown off internet forums, and get me into real trouble, whilst at the same time resolving more dog-to-dog reactivity cases than any other method we had. A technique that was to bring to CaDeLac the reputation of solving dog-to-dog reactivity cases where others had been unable to help.

As the years went by I started to encounter more and more dogs who 'went mad' when they saw another dog, or indeed 'went mad' when they got over-excited by anything they saw or heard. Even in some cases where they were terrified and trying to run away, I discovered that this technique can and did help.

It certainly isn't a technique that can be used with every dog, or by every handler. It is also a technique that poses risks to the handler, if a dog is of the type that might turn and bite its handler when it's highly aroused and the handler tries to turn it. But in its refined state, it is a technique that can and does help a lot of dogs, and halt their unnecessary reactivity to other dogs. Often very quickly and usually permanently.

Between 1977 and when I met Sabre and Linda, with lots of help from my own dogs of the time – Cassie, then Lace, then Cloud and Connor – and a host of other dogs belonging to my team of instructors, we had helped and 'cured' several dozen dogs of their reactivity issues, so when I met Linda and she told me about Sabre, I was pretty hopeful that we could help.

It was the autumn of 2008 and with the team at CaDeLac under lots of pressure to do it, we decided to run our first dog trainer and behaviourist seminar: a two-day weekend event. I wasn't really sure whether people would come, or be that interested, or whether we were good enough or experienced enough to be running such an event. With over four thousand classes under our belt and many hundreds of behaviour cases behind me, the evidence suggested that our knowledge was useful, but still I wondered if we should do it.

But we ran it anyway. The first day was all about running training classes and teaching people and dogs. The students were able to handle other people's dogs, watch classes being taken and have a go at running a class themselves if they wished. On the second day, I talked about some of my behaviour cases, the various techniques we used and the experiences I'd had. I hadn't planned to actually bring any behaviour cases in that weekend, but as it happened, the universe had other plans for me.

It was a small but very experienced, well-educated and interesting group of people that joined us, a couple of whom became good friends from that point on. One of those people was Linda.

Over lunch on the first day, Linda, munching sandwiches, told me about her dog, Sabre. A six-year-old German Shepherd, Sabre had been dog-reactive since adolescence. Linda, very well-read and as determined as any owner I have ever encountered, had gone to great lengths to try to resolve Sabre's issues and had travelled the country seeing trainers and behaviourists, several specialising in dog-to-dog reactivity. She even attended week-long courses designed specifically to help people and dogs with that specific issue. There was certainly no doubting her commitment. But despite everyone's best efforts, Sabre refused to change his ways, and was still barking and lunging and lost the plot every time he saw another dog when out on lead.

We chatted at length and in the spirit of understanding, and having taken an immediate like to her, she and I debated the various techniques she had been given by others, some of which I knew would work with some dogs but not with others. But her tale was full of failure and setbacks. Whilst she was still very keen to try to help Sabre, she had failed so often that she had almost completely lost faith. As she talked I began to sense the worrying trend of learned helplessness in her attitude. She had come to think that everything she tried would fail, or possibly make things worse.

I had heard the same story so often, the tale Linda told me that day. She had fallen foul of the terrible 'dog reactivity downward spiral' so many people with this problem will be familiar with. It starts when a dog first reacts or is seemingly 'aggressive' and an owner is worried and confused and at some point makes the decision to keep the dog on lead and away from other dogs. This usually exacerbates the problem, but is nonetheless sometimes the right and certainly politically correct and safest thing to do. She had also started to walk after dark or very early in the morning so as to avoid other dogs and thus avoid the problem, but in reality it meant that the dogs she encountered were those with the exact same reactivity problem, whose owners were also walking 'after hours' to avoid other dogs. Owning a severely dog-reactive dog can be a very lonely life and the behaviour can cause arguments with other owners; it can cause people in the locality to avoid the 'aggressive' dog and their 'irresponsible' owner. It can also cause severe injuries to both dog and handler when the dog is large and lunging is extreme. Dogs can damage both themselves and their owners' shoulders and backs, or even pull them over and drag them if they are large enough.

Sadly, dog reactivity also severely affects an owner's state of mind, their self-worth, particularly if they are otherwise knowledgeable and committed. They can begin to feel they have failed their dog, that they are 'bad' owners. That they are too dumb to resolve the issue, or simply that they are 'doomed'. I've seen cases where the owner has become under such social pressure that they have succumbed to depression or rehoming the dog, or sadly, having it put to sleep.

Luckily Linda and Sabre were both still with us, alive and well, and she was still committed to helping her dog! Though I don't think that at that stage she believed anything could be done; she had tried and failed so often. So I told her to bring the dog in the next day: behaviour day.

And so it was that Sabre came into my life. Rather unexpectedly and very publicly.

At the end of that first day we had a fish and chip supper and discussed the day's events. Conversation flowed with vigour and no one wanted to go home. What a wonderful set of delegates and potential new friends, and I was thrilled at how the team at CaDeLac had pulled together to make the day a real success. I went home, tired but elated.

When I did finally crawl exhausted into bed, I began

suddenly to have doubts. I'd never done turn and face in front of an audience before. Was it fair to the dog to do the assessment in public? I didn't know. We knew that on occasion, it didn't work. I knew that sometimes I wasn't able to help a dog in this way. And I didn't relish the prospect of failing in front of such a large and wise audience. But finally I appeased myself with thoughts that though 'turn and face', as we came to call it, might not work, there again, it might! And if it didn't then we would come up with something else, as we always did. It was a rare day that we couldn't help someone at all, and I hoped that this time, we would. If all else failed I had always said to myself that educating potential behaviourists was about teaching the highs and lows – if we failed, then that too was a valuable lesson for the delegates. The lows and tough times taught as much as the highs and the successes.

So it was that on the Sunday, Sabre arrived. As did the delegates, who were full of excitement and expectation.

When I first saw Sabre, I was impressed by his wonderful deep coat, a rich orangey-mahogany in places and deep black in others. It seemed to change colour in the light and move with his motion like waves on the sea. He looked in great physical condition. He had a handsome, pleasing face, with beautiful markings and deep-set, dark, intelligent eyes. My, he was a handsome boy! And big too! I could imagine what he looked like in full 'rage' mode, lunging at another dog. Heavily coated and well groomed, he appeared relatively at peace and at one with the world, except for a few anxious looks around at his 'mum' and the occasional typical GSD 'worry woof' in his new surroundings. With no other dogs present to distract or upset him, it was clear that Sabre had a great respect for and love of his owner. His obedience was unusually good and he glanced up at her often as she spoke. Together they looked like dog and handler at one. A bit tense at times and with fleeting moments of worry, but they looked like they understood each other very well. A wonderful and rare partnership. Despite her outward calm, I knew that poor Linda would be a mishmash of inner turmoil. Fear of failure, hope for improvement, but anxiety would reign.

Experience had taught me that the best but not exclusive chance of success with this technique is with intelligent or herding breeds. Dogs over the size of a Jack Russell and up to the size of a GSD suit it best. So this was a perfect fit for success. And if the relationship between dog and handler was good or very good, then there was a very high chance of complete success and a very fast rehab. As I watched Linda walk Sabre slowly round the car park and paddock, letting him toilet and relax, I felt more confident. I had noted that although not unfriendly, Sabre had taken very little notice of me. Another great sign. When a dog has faith in its handler, it shows a lot less interest in other people as a rule. If it has no faith in its handler then it can commonly latch on to me, or one of the team, in an effort to find someone who speaks its language better than its owner. In so doing, it totally disregards its owner. In Sabre's case his mum was the only human he was really bothered about. I felt that tingle inside when you just know that something is looking very good indeed.

It was a sunny day and we were able to use the paddock to introduce Sabre to the first of several stooges that day. The purpose at this stage was to evaluate two things: first, how bad was Sabre's reactivity and second, was he reacting out of habit, or something else?

Linda was instructed to do nothing, just hold him and let him do whatever he did.

Outdoors, the team from CaDeLac and all the course

delegates stood around the outside of the low-fenced paddock. Inside the paddock Linda allowed Sabre to sniff about and relax for a few minutes before the first dog was introduced.

I had noted that Linda held the lead firmly, but loosely, as I wanted, and Sabre was relaxed at her side. She had nodded that she was prepared. Tension and concentration were etched across Linda's face – fear, even.

At a distance of about thirty yards, from behind a door, a non-reactive, uninterested stooge, used to doing this work, was brought out of the main building to stand calmly outside the paddock where Sabre could see her.

As soon as he spotted her, Sabre gave an almighty leap and lunged forward. He barked his biggest barks, he was bouncing and leaping and I was impressed that Linda held him so well and wondered where she found the strength. Sabre in his reaction was a truly spectacular sight, like a wild and dangerous animal, protecting his space from a threat. I could clearly imagine how people who met him in the street might turn and flee, dragging their dogs away. He looked terrifying, huge, with his mouth open, his teeth showing, lips drawn back and eventually saliva streaming from his lower jaw, flying away in the breeze. He looked like a dog who would surely kill anything that came near him.

But I doubted that he truly meant it. Something about it seemed false to me.

The stooge he had reacted to was my dear Cloud. Cloud, so talented at reading dogs' intent, really wasn't very bothered at all by Sabre's most boisterous display. That confirmed what I thought.

Sabre continued to leap and lunge and bark until we removed the stooge. He calmed considerably once Cloud was gone. Linda calmed briefly too. But we had further work to do. We had established that Sabre, an entire male, had reacted to a bitch, which wasn't normal dog behaviour. How would he react to the next dog, a neutered male?

Out came the stooge and Sabre's reaction was again immediate and exactly the same as before. Leaping, lunging, snarling and barking like a demon.

We brought out a further dog, another male, and established that yes, Sabre reacted immediately and with equal ferocity to all three dogs. And now we knew exactly what we were dealing with.

Just a habit.

The fact that Sabre had reacted to the bitch, the entire dog, the neutered dog and the different breeds immediately, on sight and in *exactly* the same way, suggested that he was not reacting because he feared the dogs or saw something in them to react to, but that he was reacting purely out of habit. An automatic response that followed the visual cue of another dog. No thought, no processing, no need: just habit.

I do the same with mugs of tea. Or boxes of chocolates. I see the mug or chocolate and somehow without thinking, my arm reaches for it and lifts it to my lips. No thought involved. Just a habit!

I therefore concluded that Sabre was acting not necessarily out of any malicious intent. My soul soared as I realised that almost certainly this case was going to be a huge success, and the ingredients were perfect. The relationship between dog and owner was perfect. There was every chance that Sabre was non-aggressive, but just habitually reacting, as so many of our previous cases had been. As so many millions of dogs do.

Back indoors, we briefed Linda. We explained what we wanted her to do and how to do it. To radically alter a dog's behaviour, we must first radically alter the owner's belief system and then their habits. In the past, something that Linda had been doing, or not doing, had somehow been unintentionally supporting Sabre's habit. They had become inadvertently codependent. She was supporting him in his habit in her effort to heal him of it.

I stood in as Sabre and with a collar and lead around my own neck, showed her how we wanted her to handle Sabre when we showed him the next stooge dog. She became familiar with the collar-holding technique and we practised until it was second nature and she no longer had to think about it. A smooth, kind, fluid, calm and gentle but firm movement was all that was required. We taught her how to hold, where to hold and most importantly when to let go. I applied the technique on Sabre with no dog present and he obliged willingly and peacefully, surprised but accepting, like he might accept a vet taking his temperature.

Linda had a practice too and then we were ready to go. Back out into the paddock we went.

With everyone watching, Linda and Sabre stood once more in the paddock and it was clear that although Sabre had calmed, he was now expecting another stooge to appear. He glanced from Linda to the door, seeking her instruction, but remained fairly calm. It was the actual *sight* of the stooge that triggered his particular habit. All habits have a cue of some kind, either internal or external. Linda signalled she was ready and with Sabre now on a loose lead again, we bought out another stooge.

Sabre's immediate launch forward, barking with teeth bared, took no one by surprise. But Linda's response to his behaviour caught Sabre completely off guard. With a face fixed in concentration, detached from her emotions, calm and concentrating hard, following only the instructions we had given her, Linda reached for his collar and firmly, calmly, fluidly pulled Sabre toward her and held him close as she had been shown. Surprised by this very new and different move from Linda, Sabre's barking ceased immediately. At first he pulled back, trying to free himself to turn back to the stooge, but she held him firm. His focus switched from the stooge to Linda as he tried to evaluate what was happening to him. His habit loop was halted immediately by this surprising interruption; he was brought out of habit mode and back into thinking mode.

Sabre had been held firmly by Linda many times before – he did not fear her touch; indeed, he loved it. She had held him to groom him, to remove ticks, remove thorns from his paw, to soothe away fears of fireworks, to check for lumps and bumps, to stroke him, to massage and caress him. He loved her touch, he welcomed it, but was surprised, no doubt, that she had chosen this moment to do it. After just a few seconds held in her hands, no longer able to see the stooge from his new position, he started to relax. The moment the relaxation began, as instructed, Linda released him and he turned to face the stooge, at the end of his lead.

His reaction was once again immediate: leap, bark, leap, but Linda was fast, prepared and was already reaching again for him. She took his collar, he paused; she pulled him close, he quietened and looked up at her, again surprised, and she held him close. He calmed quickly and she released him quickly too.

He turned once more to the stooge and now, standing on a loose lead, there came a couple of half-hearted woofs, but no lunge. Linda took his collar and repeated the technique. Sabre almost looked as if he expected it. He stood calmly as she held him. He relaxed in maybe two seconds. She released and he turned once more to face the stooge.

As Sabre realised that his reactions to the stooge were bringing about an immediate, unusual, practised and calculated response from his mum, a new response that he had never experienced before, and that his efforts were becoming fruitless, he simply gazed at the stooge in a vaguely interested, slightly confused, but calm way.

We can often see a moment that defines a dog's change. It recovers from something or learns something. That moment is literally as if a penny drops. If the one thing you really understand in a situation – in Sabre's case, this was Linda – if that one constant, the one thing you really know, radically changes its behaviour, then there is a real urge to suddenly change yours too.

He stood on a loose lead, looking for a few seconds. He observed the stooge calmly, not knowing what to do. The habitual response now broken, he had no previous experience of how to behave if he could not bark and lunge. For a few seconds he looked, he sniffed the air, for the first time trying to gain information about this stooge dog. As he took time to look, to smell, to think and assess the situation, he could see for himself that *the stooge posed no threat at all. He was out of habit mode and back in the Now of things, in thinking mode. Yes! We were there!*

Linda looked down at the silent, calm dog at her side, incredulous, her mouth open in surprise. It's a face we at CaDeLac had seen often, and I looked round to see my team smiling knowingly, and many of the audience looking shocked but amazed. Tears brimmed in Linda's eyes as well as my own and in many of the onlookers'.

It is a moment that will be etched forever in my mind.

And then Sabre, glancing again at his mum, seeing her stillness and calmness, her smile, forgot the stooge, and after a shake and with a big sigh, which we see so often with this technique, he lowered his head to sniff the grass, disengaging completely from the stooge dog, and then wandered off to sniff a tree. Linda followed him in stunned silence, smiling.

As he sniffed, Linda looked at me from across the paddock through glassy, tear-filled eyes, and this was the moment when I allowed myself a big smile inside and out as I realised that together with the team of wonderful people at CaDeLac, we would in the next few minutes transform both Sabre's and Linda's lives for the better and probably forever.

Previous experience had taught me that when a dog arrives at the point where it realises its owner is no longer going to allow the barking and lunging and that the owner is behaving very differently from how they normally behave, meaning the dog must do the same, one of three things happens. The dog will disengage from the stooge dog and either focus instead on the owner, focus on the environment, or engage with the stooge in a calm, polite way, issuing friendship or play signals. Or a combination of all three.

Sabre's reaction to stooge number one had ceased and it was now possible for him to stand calmly with Linda and look at the other dog without reaction. The whole thing had been completed in about fifteen seconds. We walked the stooge about, getting closer to Sabre, but still he regarded it with only mild interest, sniffing the air and issuing calming signals to the dog. Now unworried by the dog, he focused increasingly on his owner and the environment. Linda was now smiling continuously, incredulous.

Time for stooge number two.

As soon as I mentioned the next stooge, Linda's smile fell from her face, and tension re-emerged as she went back into her habit mode. *Oh no, another dog is coming, Sabre will go wild again*, she must have thought. Once Linda was prepared, the second dog was brought out from the building and again Sabre spotted it immediately and he stepped forward on his lead, leaping, and woofed wildly. Old habits die hard. Linda was prepared and already reaching for him, held him and turned him. Sabre calmed almost at once, and once released, turned back and woofed once more, but without the same vigour and without the lunge. Linda repeated the technique and then releasing Sabre, observed him look, but not bark again at the stooge. This time I detected a slight wag of his tail and then he politely looked away a few times; he must have liked this girl, but again, he soon lost interest and focused instead on his owner.

Time for stooge number three.

As the dog came out of the door, Sabre looked up. He lifted his nose to sniff, *for the first time assessing the situation before reacting*, and he appeared to contemplate the situation momentarily, before once again returning his gaze to Linda. She smiled and praised him. Then he looked back at the stooge and he uttered a tiny, barely audible, unsure woof. Linda applied the technique, Sabre relaxed immediately and she released him. He seemed relieved. The tension seemed to have completely left his body, and then looking completely calm, he turned his attention back to Linda as she, still stunned, gazed back at him. Smiling. Calm. Amazed. Her lower jaw hung slightly, her eyes were still alight with tears.

We walked the stooge about, as Sabre and Linda both gazed on, without reaction or movement. Every few seconds he would look at Linda and she would praise him, then he would watch the stooge some more before looking back at Linda. As Sabre and Linda were now both calm and Linda beaming, I took the stooge toward them and then, asking Linda to turn away and walk off, the stooge and I followed. After a few seconds, we caught up with her and together we walked around the paddock and car park, side by side. Sabre paid no heed to the dog other than mild interest.

For the rest of the day Sabre ignored all of the dogs he encountered. We walked him up and down a few times at the side of seven different dogs and he showed no further reaction at all. Instead, at the introduction of each new dog, he simply studied them and then looked back at Linda. His habitual response had been overwritten by Linda's new behaviour and *Sabre was finding calm study of the new dogs more pleasing than leaping about the place, barking and throttling himself on the end of his lead. Sabre, it seemed, liked being calm. Most dogs do.* Occasionally he would issue communication signals to the stooge if they looked his way, but otherwise he remained owner-focused and chilled. I don't think there was ever any real malice in Sabre. I don't think most reactive dogs have malice in them. They have just somehow come to make this reactive response an automated habit.

Everyone was happy, and Sabre needed a rest, so we all filed back into the hall for a very interested and happy conversation about how this technique works, and that night every person went home happier and to ponder what they had experienced that weekend.

With Sabre's on-lead reactivity now well on the way to resolution we agreed to meet the following weekend to commence his off-lead rehabilitation work.

I can never fully describe my feelings during one of these types of cases. It looks to all intents like a work of magic has taken place, and that is how it feels. The moment when we become aware that the next few seconds of this dog's experience will transform the rest of its life, as well as its owner's, are moments that can give a real sense of purpose. For all the very sad, painful, dangerous or upsetting days one might experience in one's career working with dogs, days like this make it all worthwhile.

Before leaving I explained to Linda that the intention of turn and face is not to stop a dog from reacting to other dogs when it needs to. This was not to shut down Sabre's natural response to threatening situations or force him to ignore dogs when he really needed to act.

The purpose is to encourage the dog to pause and think *about whether a noisy, violent reaction is actually necessary. Its purpose is to stop them acting habitually and start them thinking and assessing, as most socially sophisticated dogs do. The purpose is also to change the owner's behaviour radically. To give the owner something to do that does* not *support the dog's unnecessary reactivity.*

On occasion, most dogs encounter another dog who needs telling off. If Sabre were on lead and a young adolescent, sex-crazed, overly boisterous Lab were to come into Sabre's lead space, I would expect Sabre and many other dogs, including my own, to react. I stressed the importance to Linda of showing discernment as to whether to use the technique in any given situation. But having seen Sabre's quiet relaxation following application of turn and face I fully expected him to adopt the look, think, assess and respond approach all by himself over the next two days or so, whilst retaining his 'right' and ability to tell off those that were breaching his signals or space. Linda, a confident, experienced handler, was in my view perfectly positioned to identify what was and what was not an appropriate response.

As with every case, I had instructed Linda to go out the next day and *seek out* dogs to test this on. To do everything the same as she had that Sunday, and report back to me soon. She did both things, though the report came in the form of an internet forum where she, together with another of the course delegates who had a reactive dog at home, wrote of their successes in detail. She reported that she had met eleven dogs the next day. Sabre had reacted to the first three once and once only. She had applied the technique and he had been silent for the remaining eight. She had even taken him into the vet's waiting room, a former 'no-go' area, and he had been interested in two other dogs, but had not reacted, instead lying down and observing. When we spoke on the phone she reported that both she and he now felt calmer, much more confident and actually *looked forward* to meeting new dogs.

Equal to the joy of seeing a dog transform in this way is having conversations with the animal's owners for days, weeks, even months afterward. They write, ring, email and text me so often to say they still cannot believe it is their dog. The joy in their words is clear: the relief, the freedom, the transformation. They tell me that they now *hope* to encounter lots of dogs on their walks. They tell me that their whole life has been transformed. They are walking with other dog owners and friends with dogs again. They report increased confidence, better sleep at night and a renewed sense of hope in life.

When a person loses a huge source of stress and gains the capacity to once again enjoy walks with their dog, to enjoy peace and to enjoy time together, their whole life is changed. New possibilities emerge: they can take part in dog activities that they couldn't before. They can buy a new dog if they wish, and they can once again be an accepted part of the dog-owning community. The dog is often walked more, meaning he is calmer at home. The owner falls in love again with dog ownership and starts going round motivating others to help their dogs in this way. And my world lights up for a while, with the joy and endless disbelief of an owner who one day couldn't face seeing another dog, and the next goes out looking for them. It's brilliant.

Instead of the 'reactive dog downward spiral', there is a 'no longer reactive dog upward spiral' for everyone to enjoy.

Linda wrote to me and rang me.

She still couldn't believe it, she said. Luckily for me I had enough experience of this type of dog to know that for this particular dog/owner partnership, the new beginnings of a much calmer and more enjoyable way of interacting with other dogs had only just begun.

Flushed with the success of Sabre's story so far, in such a public environment, feeling fulfilled and on-purpose, I struggled to contain my emotions and excitement. I decided that as we had just helped so many people understand reactivity in a new way at the seminar, maybe I should tell other people how easily reactivity can be resolved in some cases. Single, and alone with my elation, unable to sleep one night, I joined a new American internet forum. There I talked of our technique and Sabre's story, hoping to spread the news and to help and inspire others to overcome their reactivity difficulties.

But within two days of joining that forum I had been called a liar, a fraud, a dog-batterer and for reasons that I never understood, it was even suggested that I probably dealt with my own children in the same *heartless, cruel, violent* way that I had dealt with other *poor, frightened reactivity cases*. The fact that I don't have children seemed to pass them by. I was accused of seeing only what I wanted to see, and of being too stupid to see when I was causing damage and/or fear to a dog. In my confusion at this very hostile response, I wondered if actually I might be the things that they called me; I wondered if I and the team I worked with were wrong in some way, and if we were indeed seeing what we wanted to see. I felt lonely, confused, sad and afraid. Was I a fraud? Was I cruel? Was it just an accident that Sabre and dozens of dogs before him had been transformed? So easily, so quickly, so permanently? How could I share this technique with the wider world? What was my purpose now? Why did these people seem to hate me?

I was quickly thrown off the forum. I received a stream of private messages calling me names. I made enemies in my efforts to help. And I sank into a time of deep self-doubt and anger at the world. I had helped a lovely dog and his wonderful owner. I had brought about new possibilities for them both and I was still getting messages from Linda saying how overjoyed she was and how much calmer and happier Sabre was out on walks. And yet I was banished from a forum where I had gone to offer help. I was slandered and accused of dreadful things.

With no one at home to talk to and with no real faith in the world now, I began spiralling into confusion and self-doubt. I decided to keep turn and face a secret for now, between the team at CaDeLac and any individual who came to us for our help. I had already started to write a book about it, but I shelved it – too scared to share.

Over the years I have tried several times to talk about this technique on internet forums and with one exception, the result has always been the same. I've been yelled at, slated and called names. I've now been banned from, or felt forced to leave, most forums. But we still carry on our work with turn and face and we have similar successes to what we had with Sabre. We still transform lives on a regular basis. We have refined and perfected it further, that it may live on.

For all the pain and doubt that the internet forums brought me, luckily for me and the team at CaDeLac, the look on an owner's face when their dog just stops reacting, sighs and falls into a state of relaxation is a more powerful feeling, and is longer lasting. My heart warms each time it happens and it stays warm for a very long time. I can see that, hated or not, the team at CaDeLac can still have their hearts lit up in those moments when for one of our reactive case dogs, the penny drops and they transform in front of our very eyes.

I looked forward to the following week, to seeing Sabre again and seeing how he would cope with the ten dogs we had lined up for him to meet and walk off lead with. I felt happy and confident about that at least. We had done it so often before and had had amazing results. I hoped that Linda would once again put her trust in me and be brave enough to allow him his total freedom to act like a dog, with other dogs, for the rest of his life.

Sabre's First Off-Lead Walk

After the seminar and the work we did with Sabre we were left with just one thing still to do. Linda had kept Sabre on a lead for many years if other dogs were present, and she now had no idea how he might react off lead with other dogs. She asked if there was a way we could test it, and so we arranged to meet the next week and take Sabre out on one of our group walks, when in those days we routinely rehabbed dogs who were aggressive or fearful, off lead as well as on. We needed to see how well he could communicate off lead, and we needed to give Linda the confidence to allow Sabre off in the future, to maintain the progress we had already made and to build upon it.

When Linda arrived at my home, she looked very tense. This was normal for owners who were to face something that they wanted, but at the same time dreaded. Though Linda's confidence had grown dramatically with Sabre now non-reactive on lead, she still feared what might happen when he was let off lead with all the dogs they were to face that day.

He had had a whole week during which Linda had diligently gone out of her way to meet as many dogs as possible. Sabre had met more dogs in the previous seven days than in the previous year, and he had now learned that not reacting resulted in praise and smiles from a happy owner as well as liver cake or other yummy treats. He had also learned that most of the dogs he saw were actually quite friendly or not that interested in him anyway. Before the technique he had been so busy just barking and lunging on sight, out of habit, that he hadn't taken the time to notice that actually, most dogs are OK and don't need shouting at. He had also had time to realise that not reacting to dogs was a lot less stressful for him. Instead of hurting himself, leaping about and making a big scene, pumping up his own blood pressure and heart rate, he could in fact just walk calmly by. If he wanted he could say hi or just ignore the other dog. Either way the day went on more pleasingly without the hassle of leaping and barking. Not getting stressed out had meant that his overall levels of life stress were beginning to reduce quite considerably, because of that, he was feeling better all round!

But the most important and significant change that had come about as a result of the technique was in Linda's demeanour; her level of confidence. She was now completely sure that if at any time Sabre did react in a public place, instead of dying inside and cringing with embarrassment as most reactive dog owners do, she could simply stop it. Immediately.

There is no doubt whatsoever that the *owner's* state of mind, their inner confidence and peace and their actual behaviour when encountering other dogs, are key in triggering or not triggering reactivity.

In the last week Linda's attitude toward meeting other dogs when out walking Sabre had shifted from fear and dread to excitement and wonder. She was now delighted when she met another dog, because she knew that Sabre would almost certainly stay calm and she could feel proud of him. Every time Sabre passed another dog without a reaction her confidence grew even further, meaning that by the time they encountered the next dog both she and Sabre were feeling better. The upward spiral of calm social sophistication had begun and looked set to continue.

We sorted out rucksacks and laced up boots and set off, with Cloud heading up a group of about ten dogs, all of whom were used to working together, plus a customer's dog who was on their third walk, trying to overcome severe nervousness and nervous aggression. The walk started with a small stroll down the road, on lead, with the case dog trailing the rest of the dogs. Then came the off-lead bit that Linda must surely have been dreading.

The walks were often followed by a visit to the pub, or on rainy days a warm by the fire in my little cottage, and the dogs were happy and excited, the air filled with laughter and friendship. We set out in heavy rain with rucksacks full of human and dog food on the three and a half-hour hilly, muddy, arduous walk, through fields, across roads, across streams, over fallen trees, through a bog, and up some fairly substantial hills and down the other side. We got utterly soaked and exhausted, and stopped for sandwiches and dog biscuits in the middle of a field halfway. At the end there was a swim in a small lake for those that liked swimming to wash off all the mud.

Sabre trudged on with the rest of the group, off lead, free to interact as he wished. He wasn't a spot of bother at all and Linda kept saying, "I can't believe this is Sabre." To the team of instructors and their dogs, this was normal and what we had expected.

A few dogs had approached him and asked him to play, but he had declined by just looking at them blankly. They accepted the polite 'No thanks' and went off to find someone else to play with.

On that walk, one of the dogs that usually taught play to rehab dogs requested that Sabre play with him. Sabre had stared at him blankly in a polite decline of the offer. The other male persisted, and started to bark in Sabre's face. It all came from nowhere. One minute we were all chatting, the next a dog nearly equal in size to Sabre was barking, rudely, only inches from his face, to a dog who only one week earlier had been dog-reactive on sight to all other dogs. It looked like some sort of challenge. Linda was standing close and luckily caught it on video. This had never happened before on a group walk and suddenly I became aware of what was happening, as things went from normal, to not normal. I wondered what might happen next. None of our group of rehab dogs had ever got bolshie this way with an innocent case dog. Sabre had done nothing wrong.

Sabre politely persisted with his blank-faced approach and the barking dog persisted for several seconds, becoming closer, louder and more irritating, perhaps in an attempt to incite a game of chase? It all happened so fast that I couldn't tell. I thought about intervening, but instead I looked to see where Cloud was. As if with one thought all of the instructors turned to see what was happening and then a fraction of a second later, Cloud, who had been the far side of the large dog group, came flying in through the middle of the group, intent on splitting the interaction between Sabre and his 'opponent', and as she approached her intention was clear – to put her head between the two larger male dogs. They read her intent before she arrived and they simultaneously turned away from each other, immediately losing interest. They didn't interact again for the rest of the walk. Cloud too lost interest and the walk immediately settled down without further incident.

All went well, and the weekend after we went on another walk. The same route with more or less the same dogs, and this time it was clear that Sabre was actually pleased to see some of the dogs he had come to know. To him they represented a very long walk, the opportunity for part of a ham sandwich at the halfway mark and a very happy, smiling mum.

One of the many benefits of using other dogs to walk with dogs who have been out of off-lead social contact is that the case dog comes to see the arrival and presence of other dogs as a potential benefit; as a link to great walks, lots of owner time and the chance to just watch and learn again from other dogs, behaving in a friendly way toward them.

Having a dog like Cloud to keep the peace and quiet in a group was an utter privilege and I am so grateful to her for all that she taught me. Taught *us*.

Sadly, that group of dogs fell apart as a working pack when Cloud died. So these days we mostly use our highest-level obedience class to continue socialisation, with walks where possible with selected dogs.

Every time I see a dog split a fight or interaction I am stunned. I've seen Cloud and others do it many times, and it is almost like they are conveying their intent through their minds. It is rare, from what I have seen, that a splitting dog makes any contact. Dogs are so fantastic at reading intent that they don't usually need to make contact. I love also that after such an incident, all the parties involved just move off without further contact, as if nothing had happened.

Such is the power of a peacekeeper.

Three weeks after I originally met him, Linda brought Sabre to classes at CaDeLac. She drove him the eighty miles there and back each Wednesday evening. Sabre never caused a problem at class and their relationship was blossoming, such was her commitment. And he never uttered a bark in class that I remember. Slowly it became clear that Sabre was actually almost as good a teaching dog as Cloud was. He could read and change situations with other dogs, and slowly Linda's faith in him had become complete enough for her to begin her own group walks, with Sabre at the helm, closer to where she lived.

Sometime later she began to foster dogs, taking strange dogs into her home, and Sabre was perfectly accepting of this, though he sometimes told them off if they were being gits. But that is normal dog behaviour.

We see it so often. Dogs come into the clinic as dog-to-dog reactive. We help them stop reacting and in a short time they turn out to be brilliant teaching dogs, dogs who can communicate and split and do many of the things that Cloud could do. (Though never as effectively, in my eyes.)

Linda and I were now very firm friends and although I knew she had to go away for a while, taking Sabre with her on a personal mission, I said before she went that she was welcome to a job at CaDeLac if I had enough work for her when she returned.

And so it was that two years later Linda returned to CaDeLac, not as a customer but as a colleague and friend. A year later she was running CaDeLac, as she still is – very well. It's odd how a single event can grow and multiply in its effects.

Linda herself has made changes to the technique, introducing greater and more immediate rewards in the form of liver cake or similar. I had been mainly just using praise, and using the calmness as a reward in itself. But as I have never actually owned a dog that behaves in this way I figured she knew better than me. So if you come to CaDeLac, and we use turn and face with your dog, then the results are partly down to me and partly down to Linda.

Thank you to Linda for allowing her story to be published here, and for agreeing to retain her name in such a crucial chapter of the book.

And to Sabre, who so sadly passed away in December 2015 due to old age.

Run free, handsome boy. May your rainbow life be full

of happy dog encounters and big juicy bones. Thank you for bringing Linda into my life, and for being the most handsome case dog ever. Live forever in all of our hearts.

Linda's Story:
Sabre's First Group Walk

There is always more than one side to every story.

Whilst writing this book, the section pertaining to Sabre has been checked by Linda, for accuracy of memory. After reading through my chapter on Sabre's rehabilitation, Linda had a few things to say to me. So I asked her to write them down.

This is the story of Sabre's group walk, in Linda's own words. Thank you to Linda for sharing her side of the story.

Sabre's First Group Walk: My Experience
By Linda Shearman

But the most important and significant change that had come about as a result of the technique was in Linda's demeanour; her level of confidence. She was now completely sure that if at any time Sabre did react in a public place, instead of dying inside and cringing with embarrassment as most reactive dog owners do, she could simply stop it. Immediately.

Ha! I'm afraid on this particular morning Denise's observation of my demeanour couldn't have been further from the truth! Yes, I had gained so much more confidence with Sabre when other dogs were around; I was sure I could stop him reacting in public to other dogs... but that was on lead! With the other passing (single) dog on lead!

Today was different. Denise had said my boy would run off lead with around twelve other dogs. Yes, twelve! And yes, off lead! Dear God, the thought just made my stomach churn. On the drive up from Wolverhampton to Derbyshire I felt so very sick, as I had in the previous days leading up to it. My heart felt like it had literally moved into my throat. We packed the car up early, and set off, planning to arrive just before 10am. With each passing mile of the journey I had hoped one of several things might happen. Maybe I'd get lost (as I often did), and not make it on time. Maybe I'd get called into work. I was on call 24/7, and this often happened at times when I had important stuff planned, so why not today? As good a day as any, I thought.

Mile after mile seemed to flow by far too smoothly, and in the back of my mind I really wanted an excuse to be able to call Denise and cancel. I pulled over at the services at one point and picked up my phone.

I found Denise's number, and rehearsed the words: "I'm sorry, Denise, but sadly I can't make it."

I put my phone back on the seat next to me, and realised that I so very much wanted to see Sabre mix normally with other dogs, relax, and even, maybe, have fun. So I restarted my engine and we continued on our journey. All the time thoughts filled my mind: how much damage could Sabre actually do given the chance? He'd never been off lead with a group of dogs! How badly could he injure one of them before we could stop him? How many could he injure? He was a big, strong dog, with huge teeth and powerful jaws. Would the injuries be minor? Or worse? Even life-threatening? Oh God, what was I doing?

Before I knew it, we had arrived. I sat in my car outside Denise's house and again picked up my phone to make the excuse call. No one had seen me; I could easily slip away, and be back home in around an hour or so. Home, safe and sound, with my boy. Right now that sounded like heaven!

Instead, I opened my door, told Sabre I'd be back in a minute, and walked up to Denise's house to let her know we were here. Denise opened her door and greeted me with a big smile and a welcoming hug. After attending her weekend dog-trainers' seminar, I had gone home, totally in awe of this lovely, inspirational lady. I don't think I'd ever met anyone who had filled me with so much positivity. Little did I know at the time, but that weekend would give me the strength and motivation to make some real big, life-changing decisions. Life-changing in no uncertain terms! My life is what it is today (which is wonderful, by the way!) due to that weekend, what I learned about Sabre, about dogs, about myself, and the courage, strength and inspiration I came away with. I will always be indebted to Denise and the team at CaDeLac for that.

So we chatted for a while, as the others arrived. Denise's team, a few of her friends, and… all their dogs! Everyone was getting out of cars, bringing their dogs with them. I thought about Sabre lying in the car waiting for me. That's it, I'd made a decision. The other dogs could do their off-lead walk, and Sabre could stay on lead. Simple. I could control him, he'd be happier, and most importantly, everyone would be safe!

All too soon everyone was ready to set off. We walked out of Denise's drive, and I headed to my car, stomach doing somersaults! Denise got the others to walk slowly ahead of us, whilst she came to the car with me with her dogs.

"There's a short street walk, then we'll be there," she told me.

As I opened the boot Sabre lay patiently, as he always did, whilst I clipped on his lead, jumping out the car only once

I'd said, "OK." He really was such a good boy, in so, so many ways.

At least he didn't bark, though.

We walked at the back of the group through the beautiful little village of Ticknall, which little did I know, would one day become my home. Sabre was a little excited about being out somewhere different and was keen to sniff his new surroundings, occasionally looking up at the group of dogs in front. We turned off the main street and walked up a stone drive with little cottages either side. At the top was an old wooden gate that led out onto a field, which was then quickly followed by a mass of huge trees.

I realised that as we had walked the short walk we had gradually drawn closer to the group of owners and dogs, and by the time we reached the gate we were just yards behind the last dog. As we went through the gate Sabre began to pull. I was so wrapped up in my own tension I really wasn't sure whether it was the prospect of sniffing the unfamiliar field and woods ahead, or to get to the other dogs. I convinced myself it was the latter. I was sure he was looking at one particular dog ahead. A small, black and brown Terrier-type dog.

Once we had walked for a few minutes in the clearing, everyone started to let their dogs off. They all began running around happily sniffing, some playing chase, saying hi, then moving on to explore their surroundings.

Denise looked at me and said, "OK, unclip him." I felt my grip on the lead tighten. *What, now? Are you serious? We're only just here!* I looked at Sabre, who again appeared to have his eye on one of the smallest dogs in the group, who was now running around merrily, without a care in the world.

Sometimes we have flashbacks. At this moment I had a flashfoward! It consisted of snarling, fur flying, puncture wounds, blood, tears, etc., etc.

"Maybe in a little while," I replied to Denise.

"Just unclip his lead, it'll be fine," she said.

So I asked Sabre to sit, which he always did before we put his lead on or off – like I say, he was such a good boy. But this time, I could feel his body leaning forward; he was tense and focused on something in the distance. The little dog?

Again, I heard Denise tell me to undo his lead. Her voice sounded like it was coming from miles away. As my fingers touched the metal clip, it felt like time stood still, then a voice right next to me, loud and clear, once again said, "It'll be fine, don't worry." I held my breath and unclipped.

Sabre surged forward. Oh God! I couldn't breathe. *This is a mistake!* My hand reached out to make a grab for his collar. Too late! He was off. He charged right into the centre of the group of dogs. The other dogs had seen him coming, and as if in some perfectly rehearsed synchronised display they all stopped what they were doing, turned and looked at him, as if to say, *And your problem is…?* Everything suddenly seemed to move in slow motion. Sabre seemed to look from one to the other, maybe trying to identify the weakest link? Then he made eye contact with Denise's little Collie bitch (Cloud), who held his stare in no uncertain terms. Although this was a matter of seconds, in the slow-motion interpretation going on in my head, it seemed like forever! Suddenly, Sabre turned away and started sniffing the grass, at which point so did the other dogs – except for Cloud; she watched him a little longer. He glanced up briefly at her a couple of times, but went about his business of sniffing, as if to say, *Nope, I'm not here for trouble, honest.*

We all continued to walk, and so did the dogs. For most of the walk Sabre paid little attention to the other dogs, and they to him. He just seemed totally happy to be out and about, off lead, enjoying this new experience, checking in with me once in a while. At one point a Boxer dog did try to get him to play, which he really didn't want. And I think 'Persistence' must have been this Boxer's middle name! He was dancing around him, barking in his face and making attempts to nip playfully at him. All the time Sabre just kept turning his head away. This went on for a while, and I was totally amazed at my boy's patience with this younger dog. After a short while Cloud came towards them at speed, with a stare that said, *OK, enough now*, at which point the Boxer got the message and turned away, never bothering Sabre again after that. That was the first time I had seen Cloud split a pair of dogs. I'd even somehow gained the courage to get out my phone and film it, so I have it on record, that amazing moment.

We walked off lead for over three hours and arrived back at Denise's with very wet, muddy, tired but happy dogs, and no incidents! My boy didn't kill anyone else's dog, in fact he was just perfectly behaved, and had had the most wonderful time, as had I. Denise had put on food: a selection of meats, breads and cheeses. There was a fire flickering in the hearth. We ate and chatted, whilst many of the dogs slept in various places around her house. I felt right at home with these wonderful, understanding people, who had given me and my dog this opportunity. No judgement, no criticism, no negativity. Just acceptance, help and support.

Driving home I think I spent most of the journey glancing through my rear view mirror at my boy, now sleeping peacefully in the back. What a wonderful time we had both had. So, so proud of him. So very thankful for this day. So glad I didn't make that excuse call.

And on my face? Just about the biggest smile ever.

Linda Shearman

May the Force Be With You!

One of the things that always fascinates me is the different ways that people can view a single event. I watched a video recently via Facebook where two cats are squaring up to one another and as they commence a fight, three dogs pile in and split up the fight. The cats disengage immediately and so do the dogs and everyone goes about their business peacefully. To me it looked like a simple case of 'splitting' that I talk about in the chapter on Moon.

There is no doubt at all that some dogs have a natural propensity toward this kind of peacekeeping behaviour, sometimes within their own species and sometimes across species. People call these dogs different things: 'peacekeepers' or 'the fun police' spring to mind as naming conventions which describe the same, commonly observable behaviour.

What is most interesting to me though is the fact that so many people saw this event in so many different ways. The debate/argument/riot on Facebook that ensued exemplifies this. Some people, like me, saw it as natural splitting behaviour. Some saw it as blatant animal abuse that the humans who had filmed it didn't halt the squabbling cats. Some saw it as predatory activity on the part of the dogs, taking advantage of cats whilst they were otherwise engaged, and they considered the cats lucky to be still alive. One person said that they clearly saw one of the dogs pick up and shake one of the cats, and that the dog was a cat-killing monster. Surprisingly to me, many people backed up and endorsed this person, saying that they too had seen the dog shaking a cat. I hadn't seen this at all, so I watched the video in slow motion several times. I did not observe any dog grab or shake any cat.

So what is it about human nature, or the capacity to observe, that means the act of observing is so very unique and individual? Different backgrounds can account for some of it. But what's it about when people go on record saying they can see something (in this case a cat being shaken), when to me it is clear that no cat was shaken? What is it about other people who endorse such views? Was the cat shaken by the dog or not? Did the people who saw the cat being shaken actually see this, or were they just trying to cause a fracas? And if they saw a cat being shaken, why couldn't I see it? Were people seeing what they were expecting to see? Was I?

This is a story about when a stranger and I saw something completely differently in the behaviour of a group of dogs that were under my care.

At the time I had Cassie, a friendly, peaceful dog not given to conflict (apart from with Lace if Lace picked on her) and Lace, a confirmed people-biter. I was also caring for my friend's three Border Collies. He was a dog trainer, a good one in a lot of different ways. One of these dogs was a very assertive animal and had been seen to split up fights between humans outside pubs; would split play or aggressive displays between other dogs and was known to have bitten at least two people in defence of her owner. I will call her Jilly. She was a very talented dog indeed, and one I loved.

So amongst the five dogs, there were two that had the capacity and confidence to bite humans. All five were highly trained and obedient, and at that time, got on together reasonably well.

We had all been for a walk and it was a beautiful warm, sunny day. Returning home I filled the dogs' food bowls. The dogs waited patiently as I placed the bowls in a semi-circle on the paved area in the back garden, and then on a release command they all happily tucked in to their own bowl. There were never any food conflicts between them. Turning my back on the dogs, I went to go inside. Then I heard a low, deep growl, followed by another from a different dog, and I whirled around to see what was wrong.

There in the garden stood a stranger. A tall man in his mid-fifties, wearing a dark suit. An unusual choice of clothing on such a warm day. He was carrying a briefcase. I had no idea why he was there; he must have opened the side gate to enter the back garden of my home. I hurriedly took in the scene. Three of the dogs were just finishing their meal, whilst Jilly and Lace had stopped eating and had both turned to face the intruder and were bristling. They were making their intentions clear – they wanted this man gone. Like twin sisters they had locked their eyes onto him, their bodies had stiffened, they were both growling, Lace's lips were trembling and Jilly was taking slow, deliberate steps toward the man. It was immediately clear to me that they meant business.

My heart stopped for a moment as panic ran through me. I had never encountered a situation where two of the dogs I was in charge of were displaying such threatening gestures toward a person. I was concerned for his safety, but equally I didn't want this stranger there in my garden. What kind of person would walk into someone's back garden and stand so close to five feeding dogs? And why on earth was he there anyway?

"Please, stand perfectly still," I said to the man, hurriedly wondering what best to do.

Totally unfazed, he smiled cheerily. "Hi there!" He was seemingly oblivious to the bad intent being transmitted from the two bitches that were now, in stiff, slow objection, advancing toward him.

"Stay there," I commanded the dogs and luckily both bitches froze, but their demeanour was still full of intent, their rigidity clear. Lace was fully aroused and her hackles were up, making her look part Collie, part wild wolf. I was stunned at the beauty of this predatory stance, but it was pointed at a human who I needed to protect from their clear intention to get rid of him somehow. I didn't even know what their intention might be. I had never seen either of them do this before.

I wasn't exactly sure how best to resolve this situation. I knew that saying the dogs' names was likely to spring them into action, so I just hoped the 'stay' command held until I could get the man to go away. I'd never had two dogs stalk, with good reason, a person before. It was a complex turn to this peaceful day.

Unfazed, he continued, "Have you ever thought about what happens after this life?" His eyes fixed me with his genuine enquiry. I was guessing that he really hoped I had, but that I hadn't concluded anything. And that he might help me do so.

"I think it best if you slowly turn around and walk out of the gate the way you came. Please go slowly, otherwise the dogs might bite you," I replied, ignoring his question. I really didn't know what the dogs might do.

He in turn ignored my request. "You haven't, then?" He was still smiling, not even looking at the dogs, instead looking me square in the eye.

This time I was more assertive. "Turn around now and walk slowly out of my garden!"

Lace and Jilly, perhaps sensing my assertiveness increase, took one slow, deliberate pace toward him, in unison, as if they were a single animal with a single intent. The growling had now stopped but their menacing demeanour had increased. The silence before the storm? I could feel their tension in my own body; surely he could too?

Apparently not. He continued. "Well, I know what happens after this life. I know there is another life, a better life."

"Well, that's probably a good thing," I replied. "You might be needing another one quite soon, *if you don't leave my garden immediately!*" I nodded toward the dogs, trying to direct his attention to their menacing behaviour. Again they took another step forward. Lace lowered herself to spring at him.

"Stay there!" I again commanded them.

"Oh, I'm not going anywhere, don't worry," replied the man, assuming I was talking to him.

I simply couldn't believe the craziness of the situation. I thought that instinct made all humans fearful of advancing, snarling dogs. I know I'd have been pretty scared of them had they been stalking me in the way they now stalked him. Stiff, alert, intensity rippling through their honed bodies. This guy was nuts and the dogs were getting more serious by the second. I wasn't sure how many times they would accept my 'stay' command. A few more paces and they would be on him anyway.

I decided to be more assertive, in an attempt to save the man.

"If you do not leave my garden I will release the dogs and they *will attack you*. You have been warned. Now please leave!" Most people would be scared of the threat of two dogs attacking them, surely?

"Oh, I'm not scared of dogs, I am protected!"

Protected? By what?

Jilly, in slow motion, lifting only one paw at a time from the ground, took a further pace toward him, her body low in a stalk, her intent fixed on him, the moving paw inching just one step nearer to the man she now clearly intended to attack. They were both now within a few feet of the smiling, oblivious man.

"I know that God is on the side of those that do his work. Whilst I do his work, he will stand by me and keep me safe. I fear not the dark, nor the sinners, nor your dogs, for God is with me."

"Are you totally crazy? You are going to get yourself killed with that kind of attitude. I'm all for God helping you out, but these dogs don't know about God. Now will you please show some common sense and get out of my garden before I set the dogs on you!" I tried the direct threat.

"So you've never pondered the next life, then?"

I was becoming exasperated. The dogs sensed it and suddenly Jilly sprang forward and with a well-aimed air-snap, timed to perfection, she grabbed and tore the bottom of one trouser leg. The shredding sound it made heightened my arousal.

This wasn't my dog, and I had no idea if she might respond to me. But she did; her master had trained her well. "Jilly, leave it. Come here!" She came away a few feet but then snaked back to face him with the same menacing glower. She spat out the material that she had in her mouth and recommenced her menacing stalk. Lace still held her position about three feet from the man, frozen with intent, awaiting a command from me or a false move from him.

He didn't flinch, but he looked down at his torn trousers, then looking back up again said, "You see, God *is* protecting me!" He smiled, triumphantly.

"*Get out. Now!*"

He finally seemed to get the message and he turned to leave. The movement readied the dogs and they flinched with captured energy, wanting to spring at him.

"Stay there," I urged them again.

As he turned, he lifted up his jacket for me to see the back of his trousers. There was a large tear of material that extended from buttock down to mid-thigh. The material, somewhat shredded, hung uselessly below the tear. I observed he had dark-coloured underpants on and that the skin below his pants flamed with injury. It seemed he had upset more than just my dogs already that day.

He pointed at his own glowing bottom area, as if it wasn't obvious enough, and said, "He protected me from the German Shepherd Dog at number 14 and now he protects me here. I am living proof of God. You have borne witness to his lesson. God is here with us and he protects those that do his bidding."

"Righto!" I said, utterly incredulous. As he began to walk away I asked Lace to walk on toward him. She followed him obligingly, keen to have him leave, and then as I called her she returned to me.

I heaved a massive sigh of relief and thanked the skies above, and then I suddenly had a thought.

I wondered what might remain of his trousers after their encounter with the Rottweilers at number 42!

Cloud's Way

No book that I write could be complete without at least one story about the most intelligent, determined and influential dog I have ever known, my dearly missed Cloud.

Cloud was such a powerful and charismatic character that her various antics could probably fill a book all by themselves.

If you had to name Cloud's strongest virtue it would be determination. Her sheer bloody-minded utter commitment to have what she wanted, when she wanted it, how she wanted – no matter what effort, the barriers, or the consequences. A truly admirable trait.

Later in life she became an extraordinary communicator with other dogs and she single-pawedly reformed a large number of aggression cases; she also headed a large group of dogs who worked together to reform aggression cases, and she saved the lives of both Lace and puppy Connor.

However, she routinely endangered her own life, jumping from great heights, taking risks I'd never seen other dogs take and yet she robustly survived the most hazardous of experiences without fear and often without harm. She would split up fights between dogs much larger than herself with seemingly little effort, and she would train other dogs to cease jumping up at people, jumping up on worktops or barking unnecessarily, and she would chase dogs that had failed their recall back to their owners. Additionally she stopped inappropriate humping, as well as halting overzealous play. She also had the capacity to fix a human rigid with the intensity of her unblinking, unwavering stare. When Cloud looked at you she somehow bored straight into your soul, as if she was roving around inside your mind, steadfastly decoding your deepest mysteries and finding your vulnerabilities. You couldn't quite be sure if she felt sorry for you in a pitying kind of way and planned to help you with your 'issues', was going to 'save you', or if she was simply working out how best to get whatever she wanted from you. She gave you the impression that she could see you so clearly from the inside that she knew you better than you knew yourself. It was thoroughly unnerving for many. But over the years I grew used to it, and I took it to be a sign of love. Love seemed less menacing than control.

Later in her life she became extremely loving at times, but at first, I'm quite sure, she just thought humans were there to serve her. In many ways she was more cat than dog. A feline/slave relationship. She was also rather fox-like. More than once people said, "Wow, you have the cunning of a fox in there!" She even looked like a fox. She often seemed completely wild.

She had an unusual and natural talent for balance that I have never seen in any other dog to such a great extent. She could walk along the top of a very thin fence, much like a cat. She often stood on and walked along, if you allowed her, the back seat of the car. Like a cat, but without the claws. From a tiny puppy she would leap several times her height to get where she wanted to go, with a precision that implied an older, wiser, more nimble and supple animal. It was pure will; I believe that got her all that it got her.

There has been much written and counter-arguments made about the view that dogs are pack animals, as is the case with most canids in the wild, and/or the view that they wish to control the world, or at least the part they occupy. Many arguments have raged over whether there is such a thing as pack leaders.

One thing was clear to me and everyone who knew her when she was a puppy: Cloud wanted what Cloud wanted and one way or another, Cloud would almost certainly get it. If there were other dogs who knew her around, most would somehow seem to follow her lead, to mimic her, gain confidence in her presence and bow down to her whims and wishes.

But deep inside her, waiting to come out one day as it surely did, was the most loving, caring, self-sacrificing side, which once ignited, never left her. She was simply amazing.

In this story Cloud was around two years old and I had found myself moving house, in dream-come-true style, to my favourite part of the country, Wiltshire. I had always longed to live in Wiltshire, which I considered my spiritual home, and I had plans to start new dog-training classes and clinics in the local area, whilst leaving the main part of CaDeLac running back in the Midlands. I hoped that the area was short of dog trainers, but the move happened so fast that I had no time to research, so was just living on hope.

I am always conscious that not everyone loves dogs and wherever I live I try to keep my dogs in a way that prevents them from becoming a nuisance to others. I pick up poo and keep them on leads where they might bother others. Additionally I try to ensure that their barking and noise is kept to a minimum. I try to fit in with the views of the local community and cause the least offence wherever we go. And in this instance I was particularly keen to make a good impression with my dogs and be welcomed into the village we had chosen for our new home – possibly the place where I might start a new dog-training business.

It was a lovely village, and a beautiful little cottage at the side of a wide, tree-covered walkway, nestling like a magical, enchanted place under huge old beech trees that rustled and swayed in the breeze. It was perfect, I thought.

No sooner had we arrived in the village with our big van full of furniture than the sun came out. I read it as a great sign and I smiled a knowing smile inside. It was very hot, and to ensure that the dogs were safe whilst we carried furniture from the van up the long, thin garden to the house, I tethered both Cloud and Lace to the metal pole that supported the long washing line. It slotted into the ground via a thick block of concrete. *That should do it*, I thought. They were safely in the shade, had a bone to eat, had a bowl of water, the birds were singing, the sun shining, and the overall effect was enchanting. I loved this place. *Denise, you have come home!* I thought, and smiled once more to myself.

Cloud had always been an escape artist, so I pulled at the plastic-covered metal tether line to check its strength, and pulled at the pole. Both were solid and robust. There was no way Cloud could get free from this arrangement. The garden had a long hedge on one side, and on the other a four-foot-high wooden fence that separated us from the cottage next door, to which our new home was joined. As the garden was unsecured at the end it was important that the dogs were kept tied up when outside until I could provide adequate secure fencing to keep them in safely. Munching on bones, in the shade of a tree, the dogs relaxed and watched us unload the furniture and struggle and labour in the heat of the day, up and down the lengthy garden.

The next-door-but-one neighbour, a lovely old gentleman, called to see if we had milk or needed any help and we chatted in friendly fashion as he admired the dogs' shiny coats and relaxed attitude to life. What a lovely, friendly village this seemed to be! Everyone had been polite and with the sun shining there was real hope in my heart that this little cottage, surrounded by beautiful old trees, would perhaps bring good fortune our way and a new life of fun and exploration for a long time to come.

Revelling in his friendliness and keen to understand all I could of the villagers and their lives, I chatted at length with the kindly gentleman and in so doing learned a few very important things. Firstly, there was very little in the way of dog trainers in Wiltshire, he advised; the only one around, it seemed, lived in and operated out of this village! Damn. I had no desire to step on someone's toes. The vets here were thought to be good and had been kind to him when his last dog died. The vet who worked there most often was actually my new immediate neighbour; she lived the other side of the little wooden fence. *Brilliant*, I thought. *That's handy. You can't get much closer than next door!*

Later that day as our efforts were drawing to a close I sat down to have another tea break and take in some afternoon sun. The dogs were still munching away and seemed happy in their new garden. Then I saw a car draw up at the end of the garden. It was our new neighbour, the much-loved village vet. She got out of the car and walked towards us smiling, hand outstretched to introduce herself, and we chatted amicably for a good while. She seemed really nice.

The vet commented on how calm the dogs were and how well they looked, and I flushed with pride. I explained that the elder dog was a really great girl but that Cloud, the youngster, was a dog of such character that I never really knew what was going to happen next. I didn't give full details of all the problems Cloud had caused me: wrecking the house, the car, making me feel hopeless and useless as a dog trainer, trashing my confidence and causing me grief. I didn't mention all the unexpected things that Cloud had done: her jumping off bridges, chasing cars, fighting with a huge bull on the farm, digging a vast den in my garden, intimidating people with her knowing stares, or being the most wilful and determined dog I had ever had the pleasure to know. I kept that bit quiet, hoping that the vet would continue to consider her calm and well-mannered. Cloud in some ways was my darkest secret. She had me spinning with confusion and often left me gobsmacked at just how much rambunctiousness a single animal could cause.

My heart was warming every moment to this lovely, spiritual place, full of kindly, friendly people who liked to chat and share their happy tales of life in the village they loved. Everything was going so well.

Soon enough my neighbour went into her house, and reappeared moments later with a basket of washing, which she proceeded to hang. It was like something out of *The Darling Buds of May* – all country tales and birdsong.

As she was pegging out, she turned to me and said, "Do you know the local walks yet?" I moved toward the fence to hear her more easily and she broke off from hanging her washing to tell me how lovely and extensive the walks were. Once again my heart soared – it sounded so perfect for dogs! This was incredible: a lovely house, lovely neighbours, lovely attitudes to life, lovely walks, lovely weather – could it be any more perfect? I had visions of her and me becoming great friends. Drinking tea in the gardens together and walking over the gorgeous Wiltshire Downs, chatting happily about country affairs and animal matters. Perhaps sharing a glass of wine around one of the cottage fires in winter, chatting late into the night as the snow fell heavily outside, bending the branches of the age-old beech trees that surrounded us.

And then it happened.

As we leant over the fence chatting amicably I heard a tussle in the bushes by the fence, and then a moment later a small tabby cat leapt down into my new garden, barely a few metres from the tethered dogs. The lady vet and I saw it at the same time, and there was a moment that was frozen in time when no doubt the vet wondered how my apparently well-mannered dogs would deal with what turned out to be her beloved cat. But I knew and feared how my dogs would react.

Lace would stand and watch it; she had been trained not to chase cats. She knew exactly what was expected of her and always did the right thing. Cloud too had had training to not chase cats, much more training than any other dog I'd known, but it had made not the slightest bit of difference. Cloud clearly understood what I was trying to teach her, but she didn't want to do what I wanted her to do, so she didn't do it. As was Cloud's way. I could see her thinking, *Oh, so you don't want me to chase cats. I get that bit. But I like chasing cats so you, dear human, are out of luck!* And I knew that Cloud, as ever, would commit every ounce of energy she had to getting that cat! Lace froze as Cloud leapt forward in instant full flight as the cat, realising its mistake, started to run flat out up the garden.

Horror filled me as a I realised Cloud was going to hit the end of her six-metre line and probably hurt herself very badly, so I shouted desperately, uselessly, "Cloud, lie down!" It was her strongest command.

She ignored me completely and almost immediately she reached the end of her line, in full flight. There was a terrible crunching sound, which I thought was her neck breaking, and she somersaulted and fell heavily onto her back. I heard the wind rush out of her body as she slammed into the ground. She had in fact broken her collar, and as I dived forward to catch her, she quickly regained her feet and tore up the garden, flat out in hot pursuit of the fleeing cat, leaving me face down in the grass, my arms empty of the dog I tried to grab. *Oh no! No, Cloud, please don't.* The cat was running for its life now, at top speed up the length of the garden, skidding round the corner at the top and with the most nimble, high-speed 180-degree turn I've ever seen, she sped down the neighbour's garden toward the safety of the cat flap and her home.

Though she had badly injured her already weak neck and winded herself, Cloud was undeterred and she went full pelt after the cat, turning the corner around the fence almost as quickly as the cat had done only moments earlier. I sprang into action and tried and failed to get over the fence in one bound to intercept Cloud as the bushes made it too difficult. At the same time, the kindly lady vet had positioned herself in the centre of her garden. Having allowed the cat passage past her toward the house, she now stood like a goalkeeper in a penalty shoot-out, ready to intercept Cloud. As a vet she was used to reading animals, but still it was a surreal, almost cartoon-like moment as she stepped from side to side trying to anticipate Cloud's line of chase. She leant forward and shouted at Cloud. Cloud just ignored her presence as if she didn't exist, and taking the most direct line at top speed she ran straight through the lady's legs, in the process completely upending the desperate woman and sending her spinning to the ground. I was now finally over the bushes and the fence and was running after Cloud down the vet's garden.

The cat by now had won the race to the house and had leapt through the cat flap of the front door, a hole that, I observed thankfully, was too small for Cloud to get through. But no one had told Cloud that, so she hit the cat flap with such violence that somehow the impossible happened, and ripping both the outside and inside sections of the cat flap frame clean off the door, she was soon in the house and still in hot pursuit of the cat. Both the vet and I were now running for the door.

She flung open the door and ran into her home, screaming at Cloud as I dithered on the doorstep, not knowing whether to go in and help, or stay outside in case the pursuit came back outdoors. I figured she was an animal person and could do as much as I, so I stayed outside.

Cringing inside, I heard some terrible crashing sounds, the sound of many clattering pans falling on a tiled floor, more screaming from the enraged lady vet. Then I heard breaking glass, some more thumping sounds, and a dog running upstairs, perhaps? The vet was still screaming at Cloud, the cat started screaming too, there were some more banging and crashing sounds and then out of the corner of my eye I saw a small, furry body leap from the upstairs window.

Horrifically, the little cat had jumped out of the open window of the bedroom and was descending at free fall speed towards a bush. I ran towards the falling form as the cat slammed into the bushes and screamed in pain, as a branch punctured her side and tore skin from her little legs. As I ran to the bushes, the vet reappeared from the house and ran past me to her cat, trying to block its body with her own, as I turned to see what had happened to Cloud.

"Get hold of your bloody dog, for God's sake," she screamed at me, her face bursting with the blood flow of exertion and anger, tears pouring down her face as she tried to gently remove her injured cat from the spiky bush. Cloud was just emerging from the now-open front door with the frame of the cat flap still around her neck. Part of the wooden door still clung fiercely to the frame and still wild-eyed in predatory mode, she spotted the bleeding and broken cat now held in her owner's arms. Blood poured from the little cat's tiny body. As Cloud ran toward her I stepped across her path and thankfully, this time, I did manage to leap on her, grabbing first the cat flap around her neck and then I got another arm around her waist somehow and rugby-tackled her to the ground. I attached myself more firmly to the writhing, crazed animal I loved, as Cloud fought and struggled to free herself; the mangled frame of the cat flap cut into my chest as she squirmed and wriggled. But thankfully I held firm and despite Cloud's strongest protestations, I didn't let her go again.

I was stupefied with horror at what had happened and I could only stand and watch uselessly whilst as gently as she could, the tearful lady carried her terrified, bleeding cat to her car, and placing her gently down on the seat, she got in, and shooting me with an accusing and very angry, upset look, gently drove her cat down to her own surgery to try to save her life. After complex surgery the cat survived, which was the only blessing of the whole incident.

Despite taking flowers, wine, chocolates, expensive 'gourmet' cat food and a big apology card round to her house that night, the friendship never really blossomed after that. In fact, she never really spoke to me again, apart from when she handed me a very large vet bill for surgery that she had performed on her own cat, plus the cost of replacing the damaged ornaments and pieces of glassware, as well as the cat flap that Cloud had smashed and mangled during the pursuit. I paid the bill willingly, and added a long, rambling, best-intentions-*huge*-apologies-again letter to accompany it, more flowers, cat toys, chocolates and wine.

But it didn't seem to cement the relationship any.

Not for the first time and not for the last, Cloud had managed to 'change' things for me, and by the following weekend everyone in the village knew about the latest newcomer, a dog trainer with an uncontrollable dog! Sadly life wasn't meant to be in the little enchanted cottage, and only three months later we left the lovely village, to return to the Midlands, where Cloud, once again, made an impression in our next home...

To Cloud. Wherever you are and whatever you are up to, I hope that you are happy and pain-free and that one day we will run together once more. Run free, my baby girl. My love for you lives on and on.

On Life, Death and Rebirth

When I look back now to the story of Zak and his owner whose son had committed suicide in their house, and the resulting tragic breakdown of the owner and dog's relationship, it might be easy to think the lessons I learned then would prevent such a thing from ever happening with my own dogs. But sometimes life has a way of knocking you so far off-kilter that no lessons can help you. Something else has to intervene, sometimes something completely unexpected.

It's important to remember at all times that sometimes things happen which can so affect a person or a dog that their normal way of being ceases and a new way of being just takes over. As with Zak and his owner, they may be powerless to change things, and when negativity or darkness creeps into a life it can become all-consuming and unavoidable, at least for a time. It isn't anyone's fault; neither dog nor owner has done anything wrong.

It was 2013 and at that time I had three dogs in my life. Ten-year-old Cloud, who I have written of already as the most powerful, strong and characterful dog I have ever known and probably will ever know. I considered her my protector, my guide and often my strength. She had changed so many of my views about dog ownership and training, and she had also become key to the business that fed us, as she had an extraordinary talent with other dogs. She had been 'mother' to, and mentor and protector of, Connor and old boy Mirk. If Cloud had been a human, she would have ridden a loud Harley Davison, had 'badass' tattoos up her arms and had a harem of male admirers, yet unbeknown to her many friends she would do weekly shifts at the local homeless shelter where she would cook and serve food to hundreds of people.

Connor, who was six at the time, had always had Cloud there to guide him, to teach him and on one occasion to save his life. Connor is a lovely dog: highly biddable, sensitive, hugely trainable and friendly, as well as being very handsome indeed. Had he been human he would have had a very attractive and quiet wife, an immaculate lawn, a Sunday afternoon golfing habit, 2.4 very polite children, and everyone would have known him as the really nice chappie from down the road.

And then there was old boy Mirk. At nearly fourteen years old, a retired working sheepdog who had been on TV, he had come to live with us just three years earlier, after I had found him living in very poor conditions and close to starvation. My vet and I had suspected that he might survive only a short while, but with great medication, great food, an array of huge comfy beds and loads of love and cuddles, Mirk had surprised everyone by making a total recovery from his impoverished former conditions, and he had become everyone's favourite teddy bear dog. It was a near-miracle how I had found him, having known him five years earlier when I had tried to buy him as a still-working sheepdog. I'd loved him then, but the sale had fallen through and I'd been broken-hearted when he had been sold on to another home. Mirk was a huge, fluffy, scruffy dog with the most easy-going disposition and affable nature that everyone adored. Not terribly bright, if he had been human Mirk would have been everyone's friend, the loveable village idiot who people took pity on and gave cups of tea and cake to wherever he went. Mirk had a thing about old ladies and although he could hardly see and would otherwise never pull on his lead, he could spot an old lady from a hundred yards and would lean into his lead as best he could, in a fit of writhing, happy delirium, wagging unstably, wanting to be near them. He was adorable.

The three dogs, despite their differences, were great friends and when Mirk had fallen into a bog one day it was most touching to see that both Cloud and Connor had tried to inform me and fetch me so that I could rescue him. Mirk meanwhile seemed quite content to just lay there in the sinking sand, never seeming to worry or panic when he found himself in such self-induced situations of near death, as he so often did. One of my friends had a theory that having come from where he was before to our home, he might already think that he had died and gone to heaven, with his comfy bed, his top quality food and as many friends, admirers and hugs as any dog could wish for. Having already 'died', the prospect of death never seemed to worry him and he would happily leap off cliffs or fall into holes, or jump into water too rough for him to handle and then make very little attempt to swim, but instead just start to sink. He had come to be as happy in our home as any dog I had ever seen anywhere, so content going from food bowl to bed, with a brief stroll and lots of strokes in between.

We had all been through a very challenging few years. In 2011, my brother had died in horrific circumstances and on the same day, for reasons I never got to understand, my mother had stopped talking to me. As a result it had become difficult for me to see my father, so I had effectively lost my entire family overnight. At a time when I needed my family to share my grief, I felt completely alone in the world. At the same time, my business had begun to suffer very badly in the recession and I'd just realised that a large sum of money I had lent to a friend was not going to be paid back. We had been living off my savings, which were fast running out, and it suddenly occurred to me that in two months we would have no money left and not enough income to keep living in our home.

With no stable partner to support us during the recession and not knowing what else to do, I decided to cash in an endowment policy, which was intended as my retirement fund, and bought a motorhome. I couldn't afford storage so I sold nearly every possession I had and in an effort to reduce living costs dramatically, the three dogs and I moved into the motorhome and for the next two years, we lived almost permanently on the road, with no fixed abode. We had the luxury of a campsite two nights a week, but that was all I could afford, so the rest of the time we slept on roadsides, in car parks and in field gateways, or on lucky occasions, on the drive or in the garden of a friend. They were two years that were set to challenge and change me in almost every way.

Sometimes during freezing weather we had no water; on occasion, because my hands were too cold to change the bottle, we had no gas to provide heating or cooking. So the dogs and I half-froze to death, it seemed, under the covers of my bed. We snuggled together for warmth as I prayed for daylight and the bit of heat it might provide. Often the motorhome had problems and on occasion, because we were waiting for parts to fix it, we lived temporarily on the forecourt of a garage, unable to move or work. On one occasion, we were stranded for several days on a moor in snow followed by sub-zero temperatures, with a puncture as I couldn't free the bolt on the spare wheel, and the vehicle rescue company I was with refused to help us. With no phone signal and the weather worsening, I thought we might actually die. But we didn't.

During that time my health had suffered both mentally

and physically and my emotions were in turmoil. I felt as if I had failed the dogs. I had lost them their home and stability through stupidity. Eventually I ended up in hospital, having been taken there by strangers who had found me collapsed. I was rife with chest infection after chest infection and was eventually diagnosed as suffering from both severe depression and 'cabin fever'. The doctor explained that as far as my physical and mental health were concerned, another winter alone in the van was not advised.

Throughout all of this I had also tried and failed to re-establish a relationship with my ex-boyfriend, a relationship, it seemed, that just wasn't meant to be. So my heart too had been broken, over and over again.

Throughout this time of challenge and turmoil, two things kept me sane enough to function. First, the company and love of my three very special dogs, and secondly a truly incredible set of friends. Many of whom upended their own lives in efforts to help me, to change their gardens and homes so that I could at times seek refuge there, who listened to my endless ravings and fears of living the life I had fallen into. They allowed me to use their washing machines, their baths and they often fed me and the dogs too. They rallied round during the toughest times, and they supported and motivated and encouraged me in so many ways. A group of people so extraordinary that I am quite sure that without them, I would simply have given up and died. To them, and they know who they are, I am certain that I owe my life in more than one way! Thank you to everyone who helped me during my most difficult times.

And then, one day, completely out of the blue, came a phone call that changed everything. I was offered a job as a consultant and was to train a string of instructors over a period of several years. A more reliable, steady income, something we had not had for many years. The opportunity was taken and a month later I rented the house that I had once owned, and we once again had four walls and a roof for our protection. Things had started to look much brighter. I couldn't believe how life could change just like that! I was overjoyed and felt full of hope.

Oddly, the house we now returned to was the one that every one of my dogs had lived in. Cassie had died there, Lace had died shortly after leaving there, Cloud had come to us there as a puppy, as had Connor, and Mirk had lived there with us many years ago. Although small, it was much larger than the twenty-four by seven-foot space we had become accustomed to. It was my favourite ever home, had a fenced garden and it was a joy to be back in it. Our spirits lifted and life looked good. We celebrated in style, investing in a washing machine, which we had lived without for two years, a bed, and a host of new dog beds. I couldn't believe my luck and my soul soared as it seemed 'meant to be' that I and all the dogs should return to this much loved and missed home.

The celebration, however, was very short, as only three weeks later everything took a dramatic turn for the worse and though I could never have believed it possible, my life sunk into an even darker, deeper hole than ever before…

It was December 2013, and a normal day when I woke. It was cold, wintry and grey. As I pottered through the living room toward the door to let the dogs out for their morning ablutions, I passed the sofa behind which I knew my Cloud would be sleeping. Connor and Mirk trailed sleepily behind me and I noticed Cloud had yet to rise, so I called out, "Morning, Cloud" and walked on by. A few seconds later, when I realised that she had not come out and followed me as she normally would, I had the first inkling that something unusual was happening. Little did I know just how bad things were about to get. Cloud was the most alert, tense, powerful, intelligent, and life-changing dog I had ever known and it was most unlike her to fail to rise when she heard me come down.

I stopped in my tracks and turned around to return to the sofa to see what had delayed her. I saw her appear and take a few faltering steps toward me. Something was clearly very wrong. My heart stopped beating for a moment as I took in her pained, confused expression as she took one more step in my direction. I dashed back to her and then, as I reached out to hold her, she collapsed, missing my arm, and with a thud she fell heavily, as if drunk, onto her side and just lay there. As I reached her I could see that the whole of her front leg was grossly swollen, her paw looked like a balloon, she was heaving erratically and panting heavily and she felt hot to the touch. She was barely moving, she was barely conscious and my heart began to disintegrate inside my chest as shock took over me.

A mad dash to the vets, X-rays, IV antibiotics, IV painkillers, a day on a drip, some terrible conversations with my brilliant vet, another trip to an overnight vet and, just after midnight, the decision was taken to put my best girl to sleep. It had been just sixteen hours since I had first noticed she was ill and now she was gone. Forever. It is thought that she had contracted septicaemia from a callus that was growing on her elbow, which in itself was a result of lying down too much, because of her various skeletal problems in her neck, back, and both hips. I couldn't think about why Cloud died, I still can't easily, all I knew was that she was gone and I tore myself up as I pondered whether I had done something to cause it, or failed to do something that could have prevented it. It was the worst day of my life ever and I hope there will never be another like it.

Because it had all happened so suddenly, with no time to prepare myself or come to accept that she might leave me, as I might had she grown into old age, my dear friend Linda, who had been there for me when the needle took away her life, encouraged me to take her body home, so that I might mourn more slowly. It was a great decision and one that helped me, I'm sure.

Luckily, it was December and we were in the midst of a sub-zero spell, so her body froze solid on the sofa in the lean-to conservatory where I lay her, preventing rapid deterioration and allowing me time to spend with her cold, unmoving, but still very much Cloud-like body.

I just couldn't believe it or accept it. I couldn't think, couldn't eat, couldn't sleep and all I could do was hug her body and hold her and stroke and brush her. I sat for days in thick coats and woolly socks out there with her, and nights wrapped in a quilt, in the freezing conservatory with her frozen body on the sofa, and begged her to come back to me. I sobbed into her thick, cold ruff and I screamed and howled into the night. After a few days I began to function enough to walk, feed and care for the other dogs more carefully, but for most of that first seven days, I just clung to her body and sobbed, refusing to believe what had happened. I begged for this to be just a nightmare from which I might awake, I begged the universe to grant me the peace that she was now in, or to bring her back to me. I sobbed and screamed and howled my way through that week, as poor Connor, also lost without his mentor and protector, looked on at me from a distance – wary, worried, unsettled and frightened. I was powerless to help him. My wonderful friends once again rallied around and I had a visitor most days but mostly I just sat with Cloud and I cried. I simply could not comprehend life without my best friend Cloud, my protector, my inspiration and my strength.

And to this day, I know there is still a gaping hole in my heart where my Cloud once was. I can still feel it. A staggeringly painful, dark, festering blackness.

Seven days later, and with warmer weather on the way, threatening to defrost and decompose her beautiful body, Linda talked me into finally letting her go and Cloud had an individual cremation. I can still remember now the moment I saw her body for the last time as I handed her over to the kindly man. She returned the same day in a small wooden box which now sits proudly on my piano, beside Cassie and Lace.

Poor Connor was so confused. At six years old he had always had Cloud and her amazing social skills and strength to teach and protect him. Now it was just Connor, old boy Mirk, who was now also in his last few months, and me. None of us had even a tenth of Cloud's strength between us. Connor's response to my grief was to become elusive; he developed the habit of avoiding me completely and sleeping in another room, resting out of sight from me, and on walks he dragged or dawdled behind me, avoiding me. I wanted to hug him, to hold him, to stroke him, but he sensed the shift of energy in me, the desperation and the anger, and if I approached him, he growled at me.

With Cloud now gone and my behaviour worrying him so, he tried to get old Mirk to play and he moved out of my bedroom and decided to sleep close to Mirk instead. But dear old Mirk, lovely, affectionate and delightful as he was, was too old to learn to play. No doubt also affected by the sudden change of situation and atmosphere, he too began to age quickly and his health deteriorated.

Two months later, after running out of drugs that could help him, my heart was once again torn apart when Mirk was found to have a large tumour in his stomach, and so painfully for me he too was put to sleep, leaving only Connor and me.

Once more I had a beloved but dead dog in the conservatory but this time the grieving process had to be more hurried, as the warmer weather brought about rapid decomposition. I simply couldn't imagine how I could ever get over the loss of this wonderful old boy when I was already grieving for my beautiful, strong Cloud. His peacefulness; his gentle, loving, affable way of living life were gone forever. He too was individually cremated and once more I was presented with another wooden box to add to the collection on my piano.

I was utterly bereft.

When we had come back to the house I had thought that we had all come back to live in our favourite house and begin life again, after the challenges of the last two years in the van and all my personal losses prior to that. Now I began to obsess over the idea that we had all come back home to die. Day after day, night after night, I sat and obsessed about all the losses I had suffered in the last few years. My brother, Pete; the relationship with my mother; access to my dad; the lovely cottage we had lived in before the van years; my ex-boyfriend; most of my income; all of my savings; my health. I'd even lost four years' worth of photos of the dogs – through damp in the van and a technical glitch, most of my photographic memories were gone, most of my sanity and now, most importantly, Cloud and Mirk. And even worse than that, it seemed I was losing Connor too. I felt completely alone. I am sure he did too.

My mood, despair and grief deepened, and as they did, Connor's attitude too became very depressed. Out on walks he would walk up to strangers and try to follow them home, often making me cry, which in turn made him avoid me more. At home he would always rest away from me. He didn't want me to put his lead on, or indeed take it off, lest I touch him. He failed to respond to recall and even If I threw a ball, he would look at it with suspicion as if it was tainted somehow with my dark mood and malady. And the more he withdrew from me at a time when I needed my only remaining companion, the more I grew angry at him, angry at myself and angry with life.

Before Cloud died I had had a fabulous relationship with Connor. We had done obedience, agility and sheep work together. He did demos for me and worked with my behaviour cases. We had competed in and been placed in obedience and sheepdog competitions, and we had travelled the country doing long-distance walks.

All of that was now gone and try as I might to search for a solution, the distance between us, as he struggled to cope with my raging emotions, grew deeper every moment.

I felt I was standing in the way of a much better life for him.

One day, I felt I could take no more. The pain of the losses was killing me, and my grief and depression were clearly ruining Connor's life too and I felt powerless to do anything about it. As I looked at his sad, dejected, worried face I realised that actually we had arrived a point where I believed he would be better off without me. My mood had become so depressed that I believed everybody would be better off without me.

There were at least five people that I knew who would happily take Connor on, so having taken time to write my will to leave my business to my friend who was running it, and any money I had from sales of my possessions to whoever took on Connor, I decided to take my own life and leave Connor to a new life, with friends and dogs that he knew and loved. I had a plan to make a suicide look like a very believable accident and I was set to go…

But some of my friends and my neighbours, knowing the trouble I was in, intervened again and I found myself picked up by the police and escorted to the mental health section of a nearby hospital. With Connor sitting alone in a cold car outside and a long queue ahead of me, I discharged myself as soon as the police had gone, to take him home and come up with another plan.

In my experience with Zak and with others I had seen whose dog/human relationships had fallen into disrepair, I had noticed one thing that seemed to change things: the introduction of a third party. With Zak and his owner it had been the move up to Scotland to stay with a friend, who had been instrumental in healing the wounds and bringing a new focus to them both. In these situations, the emphasis shifts from the trouble between the two 'warring' factions to the newcomer and all the events and challenges they bring.

So the day after the suicide attempt I decided to do something for Connor; he needed some fun in his life again, and so off we went to a great breeder I knew, to get a puppy for Connor. That day, sweet, crazy, but loving little eight-week-old Karma moved into our home.

Immediately things started to improve. The laughter that came our way as little Karma bounced around the house in fits of puppy madness and fun lifted the terrible atmosphere that had prevailed. Connor took to her completely and immediately and they began a ritual of having two-hour-long play sessions each day as well as little frolics here and there. I was still deeply troubled, but I was happy to see Connor's mood lightening and slowly a little sunshine crept into my heart, if only for a few moments each day. Connor was beginning to get his joy back. He still didn't trust me much but at least he was happy at home with Karma.

But still he dragged behind me on walks. Still he failed to play with me at times and still he avoided resting or sleeping near me, and he growled if I approached him or touched him. Grooming him was a fraught experience and even removing brambles from his tail became a risky business as he did all he could to avoid my touch.

It was soon apparent that Karma too had troubles of her own, and after extensive tests little Karma was diagnosed as 'special needs', with cerebral palsy-like symptoms as well as hip dysplasia in both back legs. Because of her wobbly, crossing-over legs, we couldn't walk far or do much and whilst we waited for her to reach a suitable age for her hip surgery, and as it was winter, I decided to fill time by using a dating site in a rather half-hearted attempt to find a boyfriend.

And so it was that I got talking to a guy called Simon. We chatted online and then on the phone. He seemed so kind and he loved dogs. And so it was that the day after Karma's hip operation, Simon, whom I had never actually met, came to visit us. I had explained the situation, and that after the op I would be stranded indoors caring for Karma and would welcome the company. And so it came to be that on my request, so as not to disturb Karma's rest by knocking on the door, Simon, who I was meeting for the first time, walked through my door as I held little Karma still, keeping her calm, protecting her wound.

As the door opened it was like the sun had come out. Connor leapt forward joyfully with a ball. Visitors he knew could usually be encouraged into throwing his ball. Ball in mouth, he dropped it at Simon's feet, as if he was a long-lost friend returning from a year-long journey. Simon responded obligingly, then came to my side to help me still Karma, excited by his entrance, by stroking her and soothing her. It was clear that this man had a way with animals! Calm, gentle, kind and knowledgeable, he had owned more dogs than me and had a natural, soothing approach that Connor and Karma immediately loved.

The whole focus of energy shifted perceptibly as we all turned to Simon for new input. Simon took to both dogs like they were his own children and each dog responded in kind to him. And now there was a new focus for me too.

We just got on. All of us. Connor now had both Karma and Simon to love. I had the three of them, and Karma just carried on loving everyone and everything as she always had.

Three weeks later when Karma was stronger and more stable, Simon brought six-year-old Cherry, his Labrador, to visit, and after a few minor scuffles on the first day it soon became clear that this doggy threesome was also going to work very well. Cherry seemed to recognise Karma's special nature and began to mother her. Connor taught Cherry the art of dog play. The two older dogs got competitive over who was fastest and fetched the ball the best, and life was beginning to blossom again.

And bit by bit, day by day, as Connor had more and more fun playing with and lying next to Simon, he started to get less growly and more relaxed with me. As my thoughts and focus shifted from the recent traumatic past, to the future and what it might hold, my mood brightened perceptibly. Connor sensed it and he stopped grumbling so much, and he moved himself back into the bedroom we had once shared. It was not a convenient time for him to move back into the bedroom, but we welcomed him back anyway. I had missed his gentle snoring. The improvements built on one another every day until one day, just as Zak had done with his owner, Connor made up his mind that he and I should once again be friends.

In a moment that caught me by delighted surprise and which I will always remember, he got up, walked slowly toward me as I sat on the floor by the fire, and he reached out a wet, gentle tongue, and slowly, thoroughly, began to wash my face. It was almost exactly a year since he had last sought any contact with me. Since the day Cloud had died. My heart flipped and bounded like a spring lamb.

These days Connor and I are closer than we ever have been. Perhaps because of the losses and hardships that we suffered together, we are now better friends than ever. He is back to his old self in terms of his play and work and I am back to realising that Connor, although not much use as a support when you are grieving, is in fact the best dog in the whole wide world. And the threesome of Connor, Karma and Cherry is almost as happy a group of dogs as Cloud, Mirk and Connor once were.

Simon asked me to marry him, the same weekend that he brought Cherry to visit, just three weeks after we met. Ten months later, in dream-come-true style, we got married on the beautiful Isles of Scilly.

All three dogs were in attendance immediately after the service and I like to think that Cassie, Lace, Cloud and Mirk were also with us on our happiest day, and that the rainbow that we saw that night was a sign from them that they approved.

There will never be another Cloud or indeed another Mirk, Cassie or Lace, but at least now I have my Connor back and little Karma and Cherry too, to make me whole again. Plus a new brilliant best friend – my now husband, Simon – together with his wonderfully kind and supportive family.

My forty-eight years of being mostly single and living alone had also come to an end. Life had, once again it seemed, come full circle. And a new, much brighter chapter of our lives has begun for me, Connor and Karma.

To my amazing girl Cloud and gorgeous teddy-bear boy Mirk, and Cassie and Lace before them, thank you for all that you were and all that you will always be to me. Thank you for teaching me and for loving me and for living on, inside of me. You live, and will be loved, forever in my heart.

Run free. xxx

Acknowledgements

Over the many years that I have been involved with dogs, my character and life views have been challenged, changed and tested, time and time again. Each time my self-belief was questioned and had doubt thrown upon it. I battled with my own inner fears, as we all do, but mostly, overall, I came out on top.

My life, like many others, has been an up-and-down process of joy and sadness, success and failure, security and angst. It has been littered with incredible highs and terrible, stifling lows.

Throughout this time I have been truly blessed with an incredible array of extraordinarily supportive and generous friends, family and neighbours, to whom I now give thanks.

Firstly my thanks must go to Linda Shearman for stepping in and running CaDeLac when things got really bad for me, when I had lost nearly everything and had no home. For keeping me in line and providing seemingly endless support and love. For being there when my Cloud died and for steering me back to sanity when things were at their worst. You are amazing. I simply wouldn't have got through it all without you!

Also to Linda and to Daz at DZimages for the beautiful front cover design. It's stunning! On that we can all agree.

To Liz Roberts, for her tireless and seemingly endless

commitment to our friendship through the sun and the rain, the laughter and the pain. Your endlessly optimistic attitude and dependable nature have kept me going and continue to inspire me every day. I thank you with every cell I have. Without you and your calm wisdom and encouragement, I'm not sure what might have happened.

To Isabel Rowland, one of my longest-suffering friends, for years and years of committed friendship and endless support and encouragement through all those years, but especially the 'van years'. Thank you for making a new drive for my motorhome to pitch up on, providing shelter for us from the storms, for lending me your washing machine and bath. Sorry I broke your tumble drier.

To Helen, my sister-in-law. Thank you for your support and love after Pete's death and the darkness that followed, and for giving me and the dogs a roof when there was nowhere else to go.

To Keith Garner, for our endless late-night chats about life. For levelling me out and urging me on, and being there when little Karma and I were in a pickle. Your friendship and support drew me out of a hole and you brought me back to life. I cannot thank you enough!

To Nigel D. C. Hancock. For befriending me, supporting me, listening to me and restoring my faith in humankind. You are a true gent and an inspiration to many. Thank you for giving me away at my wedding. You are amazing.

To Alan and Lisa Crich, for being solid rocks for so many years and providing me with refuge during the van years. For helping me with so many things and being there day and night so very many times.

To Helen Bowcott, for her endless commitment to our friendship over more years than I care to remember.

To Sue and Jo Hallifield, for all your love and support for

so often through good and bad, happy and sad. For providing me with a safe haven to park up in the worst of weather, your endless kindness and generosity and the best Christmas dinner I ever had! Thank you for entrusting me with your sheep.

To Thomas Longton, for being a great friend for many years and for introducing me to sheepdog training and the happiest dog-training times of my life: those with Cloud, Connor and Mirk. And thank you for lending me your yard to park up, your water and electricity, shower and toilet. Refuge is priceless.

To Matt Russell, who straightened my head out Sunday after Sunday, for over a year, thank you for your patience and persistence and your never-ending support and friendship. And for your electricity and your bath! I am cleaner and wiser because of you.

To Andrew and Helen Riches, for walking with me, talking with me and making me realise that life was worth the struggle. You are an inspiration in every way.

To Mark Hithersay. You did the right thing that day! Thank you! And thank you for the photos of the dogs, the only ones I have left of them. They are utterly priceless!

To Tom Fortes Mayer, for being there, for providing your wonderful insights into how to live life to the full and for the introduction to meditation that has at times brought to me great clarity, understanding and peace. A refuge from the pain and the chaos.

To one of my most ardent supporters, Chris and John Warner. I thank you both for your moral support throughout the writing of this book – you have been stoic in your unfailing motivation and kindness. It will never be forgotten.

Thank you also to all of the dog trainers and behaviour experts who have inspired me and taught me over the years, those that have helped with my dogs and helped me see the light in times of confusion. Thank you for your knowledge, your support and your inspiration.

To all my neighbours and friends in the village who looked out for me, helped me, and even saved me, at my darkest time. To Louise, Brandon, Andy, Nigel, Kerry and Di, a massive thank you. I'm not sure what I would have done without knowing you were there.

A very special mention of my dear friend, Joanne Chalmers, who so sadly recently lost her life to sudden illness. You looked after little Karma as a puppy when I needed to work. What a wonderful aunty you were to her. RIP Jo. We miss you so.

To Sarah Smith of Charwell Proof Plus Proofreading, for trawling through my typos and ramblings and transforming the text into readable sense. Thank you for your tireless efforts and your endless support and friendship. Could not have done it without you!

To the whole team at Matador publishing, thank you for all your hard work, timeliness, your professionalism, experience and skill throughout the whole publishing process.

To Matt Malyan, a huge thank you for the superb photographs inside the book and for capturing moments so precious to me, Sabre's group walk, as well as my beautiful Cloud and Lace.

To the team at CaDeLac, past and present, and all their dogs, for helping me and befriending me, but also for your tireless work with dogs and people that needed help. To Linda Shearman, Clare Rowe, Annie Finlay, Carol Batters, Kerry Albiston and Abbie Holmes, thank you for running CaDeLac without me whilst I wrote this book. You are all extraordinary in your commitment to dogs and their owners, and in your support of me and of each other. What a fabulous place to work!

To those that influenced the way CaDeLac was run in times gone by, and who were a source of great inspiration, friendship and support: Karen Fone, Amanda Leek, Kirstin Kerr, Fiona Blackshaw, Julia Becker, Wal Becker, Jo Tether, Michelle Law, Toni Malin, Siobhan, Deb Lowther, Jazz, Matt Russell and all those from years ago, thank you for your friendship, your expertise, and all your contributions and knowledge, which has helped CaDeLac to be so well thought off and to grow. To Deb and Colin Lowther, for all the laughs, and the kindness and generosity during my lost years and for giving me refuge in your field.

To some very special online friends who have offered me help and supportive words through my losses and various challenges, I thank you all.

To my incredible vet, Carol Boothroyd, and all at Riverside Veterinary, thank you for years of superb veterinary attention for all seven of my dogs. Your support and professionalism have been second to none. Please, never retire.

To my wonderful husband Simon, for encouraging me and supporting me throughout our time together. For giving me your peace and calmness and for making me see though the challenges that love is indeed all around me. And for being so much a part of me that it is now hard to distinguish where you end and I begin. And to Simon's family, my new in-laws, thank you for reading the chapters one by one and for steadfastly encouraging this endeavour as you have. For loving me, supporting me and entrusting me with your son.

To my own family, my amazing brother Pete (RIP) who inspired in me the capacity to try to find the humour in the darkness, to stay committed to truth and light and to show compassion no matter what one's personal pain. You were the greatest inspiration that I ever had! And to my parents who gave to me this life I have led, who taught me right from wrong, gave me the freedom to be who I am, and for supporting me and loving me in your own ways. And to my dad, thank you for inspiring me to write as you did.

But most of all I would like to thank all the dogs. My very own Cassie, Lace, Cloud and Mirk, who live on in their own rainbow world, but also forever in my heart. Thank you for teaching me, for forgiving my mistakes, for protecting me and for loving me. I miss you all so much it hurts.

To Connor, Karma and Cherry, who are still in this world, still loving me, still challenging me and teaching me. Thank you for inspiring me daily, and for wagging your tails when we have been apart. You live in me, and *are* me.

And to all the dogs and owners who feature in this book, and the many dogs who have come my way in this life, thank you for teaching me and for bringing understanding where there was none.

And lastly, to all of the readers of this book. For giving me reason to write and relive some of the amazing stories of my past, and for providing opportunity to bring back to life the memories of my wonderful dogs of old, as well as some of the amazing people and dogs from my past.

If there is anyone who I have forgotten, I apologise, but if you have ever been there for me, or helped me in anyway, then you are part of me and this book. Thank you.

Over the years I have come to realise that a person is not just a person, but the sum total of all the people one has ever known and all the experiences one has ever had. I must surely be the luckiest person alive to have been granted such wonderful support in the friends and the families that have surrounded me. And to have been given the chance to spend time with some truly extraordinary dogs and their owners.

I thank you all. And love you all.

Denise x

Acknowledgements

This book is dedicated to the memory of my brother, Pete, who lost his struggle with life after a lifetime of illness. Compassion, kindness, strength and love flowed from you into the world. I hope that you are pain-free and know how much you are loved and missed. Rest in peace, my amazing bro. I loved you and always will. x

Appendix:
Turn and Face Technique

Please read this entire chapter at least once before trying the technique on any dog

Do You Have a Reactive Dog? Or Do You Work With Them?

The purpose of this section is not to provide a definitive guide of how to or how not to, use the 'turn and face' technique. That is beyond the scope of this book. I am keen however, to offer some helpful hints to those that feel that they have gathered enough information from what they've read and feel that they want to try this technique. I hope that this gives enough information for those **already experienced and familiar with dog behaviour,** who feel that they might benefit from the technique's immediate use. In addition, CaDeLac is creating a video library of reactive case dogs and will be holding a workshop demonstrating its use. Date to be confirmed at time of writing.

If you decide that your dog is like Sabre and you want to give this technique a try with you own dog, or you work in dog behaviour and wish to add this to your toolkit of techniques, then there are a few important things to remember.

If you do decide to try this technique, then you do so, entirely at your own risk.

Before using this technique in any way, please ensure that your dog's collar is strong, safe and cannot be pulled over its ears or off its head. Likewise that its lead is strong and the stitching and clip mechanism is checked for safety and security. If the collar will not stay on your dog as you pull very firmly on the collar, then do not use this technique.

This technique needs to be performed with the dog wearing a collar, not a harness. A second lead can be clipped onto a harness for security if your dog wears a harness.

I have tried as best I can to provide the essential information that will assist you with this process, but my recommendation is that it is important that you first try this technique in the presence of an experienced professional dog trainer, in a controlled environment, where no unknown or unsecured dogs are present.

It is crucial that you make yourself and the reactive dog familiar with the technique before you introduce any stooge dogs. If the reactive dog arrives at a place of calm relaxation whilst you hold its collar during practice runs, then the next most important stage is that you try the technique in the presence of a non-reactive, calm stooge dog, not an unfamiliar dog.

The most important thing is that you will need to start the use of this technique, in a controlled environment. Initially, expose only to calm, non-reactive stooge dogs that are secured on leads and in the first stages and until your dog is calm in the presence of at least 3 dogs, the stooge dogs must be no closer than 5 metres away.

In clinic, we use several stooge dogs and we ensure that the reactive dog has become non-reactive in this environment, before the technique is tried in any public place in the presence of unknown or unsecured dogs. You must do the same.

It is best to repeat the technique in the presence of several stooge dogs before you try it in a public place. If the dog does not calm in the presence of all the stooge dogs, then do not try this technique in any public place. It does not work with every dog and without seeing your dog I cannot know if it will work with yours!

There is a huge array of levels of reactivity, without seeing and fully assessing your dog, it is impossible for me to know how well it will work for you. All of my reactivity cases are assessed in clinic, we use trained stooge dogs for the beginning of the technique, we have a fence between the stooge and the reactive dog or two handlers holding two separate leads which are fixed onto two separate collars, to ensure that if a collar or lead breaks there is a second point of safety – the second lead and collar.

It is very important that whilst any dog is held in the technique position, that the stooge stands still during the first exposure to 3 separate stooge dogs.

Do not allow a stooge dog to draw nearer to the reactive dog, whilst the dog is being calmed in the technique holding position. It is vital that the reactive dog comes to trust that you have a way of stopping the stooge dog from coming closer whilst the reactive dog is facing you and has its back to the stooge dog.

I strongly urge you to read the chapter on Sabre at least twice before you attempt to use this technique. Whilst it is a simple process once you are familiar with it, it is not simple process if you are not!

When not to use it and when it won't work

It is not recommended that this technique be started in a public place or with unknown or unreliable, or un-secured stooge dogs.

It is not safe to use on any dog that may bite its

owner. If a dog has ever shown any aggression to any human (without a jolly good reason), or has redirected its aggression on to its lead or any other article, do not use this technique.

If a dog has recently come out of rescue so it is therefore unknown whether this dog is likely to bite, do not use this technique.

It works best if the relationship between dog and handler is such that the dog trusts their owner fully and is happy and used to them handling the dog, to groom, or check over regularly, or trim nails. If a dog is unhappy with any action an owner performs on its body or head, do not use this technique.

If a reactive dog is reacting to dogs, thereby 'practising' the behaviours in any other situation e.g. from behind a window, fence or gate at home, from inside its kennel or run, from the outside of an agility ring or flyball ring, or any other situation, then the chances of turn and face being successful are severely diminished to the point of making it not valid. Do not use this technique.

If the dog is unresponsive to the owner in a nonreactive situation then it is unlikely that it will trust the owner's change of behaviour enough to adopt a change itself. Do not use this technique.

If you are not familiar enough with dog behaviour to be able to decipher or understand the importance of timing, then there is no shame in that. It's a complex thing. But I would therefore recommend that you don't try this technique.

If the owner does not have the time or ability to go out immediately after turn and face has been introduced in the presence of stooge dogs where it has ceased reacting, and meet several other dogs and use turn and face then the benefits of it will be completely lost. If you are working in dog behaviour and deal with reactive dogs, then remember that unless the follow up days are adhered to, the dog will return to its old habit loop the very next day. After implementation turn and face must be used immediately any reaction is shown to another dog *unless* the reactivity is warranted, as the case of a dog running into the case dog's space whist it is on lead, or where another dog comes over and attacks the case dog.

It is the inappropriate timing of food delivery, or the use of food to try to distract a reacting dog, which is one of the causes of repetitive, habit-based reactivity. Many cases we see have been where the dog has inadvertently been taught to react, by mistimed positive associations. If you are not good at timing, then this technique is probably not suited to you. Get some help.

Remember that with all behaviours that you wish to diminish or halt, the process is the same:

1. Stop the behaviour dead, using a suitable technique.
2. Wait for a desirable alternative behaviour to occur, or prompt or guide a suitable alternative.
3. Reward the alternative behaviour.

Do not inadvertently reward the behaviour you do not want. You must not use food or toys or praise or any other positive associations until the behaviour you want to dissolve has stopped completely. Inappropriate timing of reward delivery will encourage the wrong behaviour.

Do not use food, toys or any other positive association before the dog reacts, whilst it reacts, or whilst it is in a state that looks as if it might still react. Wait until the dog changes its behaviour completely, and either engages with the owner, engages with the environment, or engages with the stooge dog in a friendly or playful way.

When it will work and when and how to use it

It works best where there is already a good relationship between dog and owner. If the owner has had success in teaching several commands already with a fairly reliable rate of response, that is a good indicator of a good two way understanding. Those that have trained for or competed in any dog training discipline are ideal, because that is a good indicator of successful communication between dog and owner.

It is imperative that the owner is strong enough to hold the dog, physically, whilst it is in a state of high arousal. The first attempts at the technique should be away from the stimulation of another dog being present, so that the dog can becomes familiar with the technique and any strong objections ironed out.

There is no doubt that with most dogs, the first and maybe first few applications of the technique are ugly to see. And sadly, it's not always pleasant for someone else to watch. The dog may pull away strongly, might shake its head to free itself of the grip, it might bring up its front paws and try to remove the owner's hands to free itself. Alternatively it may try to spin its head around over the owner's wrists in order to still see and react to the stooge dog. Stopping visual contact with the stooge is important to the process as it's this that gives the brain a break from the reaction habit loop, and the owner must use their wrists to realign the dogs head away from the stooge and into the owner's thighs, calves or groin.

Other people who witness it might lodge objections and call the handler bad names if the activity is performed in public, which is why the first few applications should be done in a controlled environment and with an experienced trainer present. I wish I had found a better or more elegant way to approach it, but so far I haven't. What is important to remember is that if a case of reactivity is so severe that it is impinging heavily on the enjoyment a dog or owner gets from their life, if their exercise is restricted, stress surrounds their every outing, danger or damage is present or being caused, then in my view most owners are accepting of the short term 'No pain, no gain' philosophy if the chances of a complete rehab are high.

A formal assessment is made before we use this technique so we are not stressing out a dog without there being a high likelihood of very significant and immediate overall benefit to the dog and owner.

In my caseload I have estimated that around 80% of reactive dogs that I see are suitable for this technique and of those 80% will have a 100%, or at least 90% overall change in behaviour within just a few days. Those that fail usually do so because the owner can not commit two days to go out and search for dogs to work with or because the dog has other opportunities to react, at the garden gate or a window, in the car or elsewhere, where the application of turn and face is not possible.

It is different aspects of the process that affect each dog differently. For some dogs I am quite certain that the holding by the owner, in itself, is part of the therapeutic benefit. So whilst it may look ugly, it is the act itself of the owner taking decisive and firm action that benefits the dog.

We stress to the owner that the thought in their head when they are turning and holding the dog's collar must be, 'Oh mate, don't worry, don't look at the dog if it upsets you! I'll keep an eye on it' (the reactive dog's back is turned to the stooge, but the owner can still see it). The attitude of the owner must be one of protecting their dog from the upset of the nearby dog. This is not punishing a dog, or trying to intimidate, frighten or hurt it. This is support that we are offering: a big hug. And that 'hugging' attitude is crucial to success. In much the same way as you might hug or hold a frightened or hysterical child, you are keeping them close until they are calmed and then you let them go to see if they can cope with the 'thing' again. *If* they become hysterical again, you hug them again. If they remain calm, you leave them be and tell them how well they have done (praise and reward them).

It is important to remember that after the first three or four applications of the technique and in Sabre's case, only two applications, the dog usually ceases the battle against the owner holding him and a calm acceptance occurs, as a dog might calmly accept a thermometer up its bum if it has happened five times already that day, during treatment in the vets.

That state of *calm acceptance* is what we are looking to achieve with the technique. When the dog calmly accepts its owner's behaviour in using the technique, it also comes to calmly accept the presence of the other dog. Calm acceptance allows for new approaches to dealing with a situation.

I consider it similar to giving vaccinations or putting a dog through surgery. If there is a high chance of overall and significant benefit to the dog and owner, then the choice to put it through short term worry or challenges is, if the owner agrees, valid. If there is no or limited chance of success then we don't try it, we opt for other techniques.

It is important to remember that holding a dog's collar incorrectly for any reason can cause pain and/or suffocation. When holding the dog's collar during this technique, the handler should exert a slight downward pressure via the collar on the back of the dog's neck, to ensure that the collar is at its loosest around the dog's throat and windpipe. DO NOT ATTEMPT to lift your dog up by its collar, as this will cause harm and pain and

potentially suffocate the dog. There is a slight pressure down, not up, on the dog's collar onto its neck. We are most certainly not trying to hurt or frighten, or suffocate an animal. What we are trying to do is stop it from seeing the trigger stooge dog by bringing its muzzle in towards the handler's thighs, groin or calves. We are giving its brain a break from the stimulus. We are waiting until it has relaxed into the situation of being held, making it realise that the owner's behaviour in the presence of new dogs has changed and that the handler is now dealing with things differently.

When a dog has been well and routinely handled by its owner in previous circumstances then it will most often relax into the situation very quickly, because it is used to relaxing in the owner's hands. The touch of the owner actually begins the relaxation process in many dogs.

Don't talk to or touch the dog in any other way, other than the application of the technique, *until* the dog's reaction ceases and then give big, but calm praise. Reward immediately **after reactivity has ceased.** Touching or talking during application of the technique will only hinder the dog's learning (could you learn something new, or read from a book, whilst I was talking to you or rubbing your ears?).

Part of the process is that the dog learns to take more notice of the changed behaviour of the owner. Before the technique, the owner is often muddled about what to do when they encounter another dog. After training in the technique, the owner is much more clear and will appear to the dog as more confident and therefore worthy of mimicking.

Before anyone performs the technique on any dog I highly recommend that they practise on a person. In my clinic's cases, I am the person who wears a collar and lead so that the owner can get used to using the technique and practise it plenty before trying it with a dog. In that way I am the one who can ensure that the owner is not applying pressure to my windpipe or throat. This action should be practised on a human until the handler is fully conversant with it.

The main reason that this technique is successful is that we do it in a clinic environment, with stooge dogs that are familiar with their role, and we have time to understand and calm the dog beforehand. We make time to introduce several stooge dogs in the first session and ensure that the owner is fully confident about its use, once out and about at home. In techno speak, we begin the 'generalisation process' before the dog leaves clinic, and the owner continues it for the following few days.

In clinic cases the dog will have ceased all reactivity to all dogs before it leaves clinic. This usually only takes a few minutes once the technique is understood and applied. From that point forward, the emphasis is on the owner to arrange their own set-up situations and use the turn and face technique on every occasion that the dog begins to react. The reactions to other dogs should diminish very rapidly, with virtually zero reaction to any dog expected by day three.

If you have a reactive dog and you fancy trying this technique out then please try to arrange to borrow friends' non-reactive dogs to use as stooges. It's not a great idea to attempt it in the street, with strange dogs until you are fully familiar with the process and have seen that it is working for your dog.

The more stooges that are introduced on day 1 the better. During the two days after first application of the technique the owner must go out and actively search for dogs. They must adhere to the turn and face technique on every occasion and at the very first stage of reaction. Usually, the reactivity will cease altogether either in the first hour of walking on either day 2 or day 3. That is normal. If it isn't at 90% – 100% reduction at the end of day 3 or after 10 separate dog encounters, then it is not working! Stop using the technique and get some help.

And always remember, the purpose of turn and face is not to stop a dog barking at, or reacting to, all other dogs. There will still be occasions when a dog like Sabre will bark at others when on-lead. That is normal dog behaviour. Sabre may at times need to tell off a rude or obnoxious or young boisterous dog who has arrived uninvited in his personal space. That would be a very different behaviour from that of barking at everything with four legs, on sight, at huge distances.

If you have read through the relevant chapters and you cannot see how this technique can work, or you are muddled or confused about it in any way, then please do not use it. To some experienced with dogs, it will seem logical, they will be able to understand the process, see how it is likely to work, and feel that it will work for their dog. If you cannot, then please feel no shame, but do not try the technique. Seek help.

And finally, **the purpose of turn and face is to teach the dog that the best thing to do in the event of an oncoming dog is to pause and have a think. Assess the situation and decide what action to take. To look at your owner and take guidance from them.** Sabre, when he first came to see us, was simply on autopilot. He was doing it because that's what he does. He wasn't thinking it through, he was just reacting. I bet if we had bought a stuffed dog-shaped toy out that day he would have reacted to that too! There are plenty of dogs that do! Using a stuffed dog-shaped toy is a commonly accepted assessment technique used by lots of behaviour folk. The dogs see what looks like a dog, they behave a certain way. They just don't think what they are doing. When they get stuck in this habit loop it's hard for them to break free. They don't appear to know they *can* break free. Until something one day interrupts their efforts and in so doing, helps them to see that.

Once we find a way of talking to them, anything is achievable.

All reactivity is on a scale of severity. All cases of reactivity have slightly different causes. All dogs react slightly differently to this technique. I cannot tell you if your dog will react well to this technique or not. If I could see and assess all reactive dogs, all of your dogs, and help you all with them, I would, but I cannot. In providing this information I have given some experienced individuals an opportunity to change their dog's behaviour. But if you are in any doubt, having read these chapters, then please do not use this. Seek further help.

Please note. If you choose to try this technique, then you do so entirely at your own risk!

I have created a group on facebook which is called "Reactive dog – Help and Support" Please join us there if you are planning to use this technique.

Caring for the stooge dogs

Whenever using stooge dogs, remember that they are the *most important* part of this process and must be respected and cared for as such! They must be happy to stand around and be barked at. Deaf dogs are often great stooges. When doing this in clinic we ensure the case dogs wears a flat collar and lead that has been checked for size. It must not be able to slip over the dog's head when the collar is pulled. We also normally ensure that the case dog is contained in a separate secure area (in our case the paddock) with the stooge outside of the fence. Or in other cases we have a second lead, usually a long slip lead, in place on the case dog and held loosely by a second handler to ensure that in the event of the collar or lead breaking, the case dog is still secured and cannot approach or harm the stooge dog.

If possible, have a fence between the stooge dog and the case dog, for the comfort of the stooge.

If any stooge dog looks uncomfortable then respect that and let the dog get away to rest and recover. Many dogs cannot handle exposure to reactive dogs and it is crucial that only suitable characters are used for the process. Allow the stooge to decide for itself if it wishes to be involved. Making sure the stooges are happy is the most important part of the process. Without stooges there can be no rehab.

My own dog Connor refused to do any stooge work the day after Cloud died and has never done any since. That is his choice and it will always be respected.

★ ★ ★ ★ ★

And finally...

Unfortunately, at the time of writing we are no longer able to do group walks in the way that we did when Cloud was alive. When she died the pack of dogs broke up, and has never really reformed into a cohesive group. Some dogs have since died and others have come in. None want the job of leader at the helm, it seems. So these days we use our top level obedience class, High school, to do the group socialising rehab when it is necessary. So a massive thank you to you people and dogs of High school, for making so many dogs so much happier. It's made possible because of you!

Interestingly, we have found that there is actually very little correlation between dogs that bark, apparently aggressively, on-lead, to how they behave off-lead. Many on-lead reactive dogs are not unfriendly or reactive off-lead. We have separate assessment processes to assess the off-lead behaviour that is not covered or defined anywhere in this book. Again this process will be covered as necessary in a future publication. I apologise for not being able to give in-depth information here, but that falls outside of the remit of this book.

If you are interested in observing or learning the technique then from time to time, if demand dictates it, we do run reactivity events and workshops. Please watch our website for announced dates.

Without the team at CaDeLac, past and present, dogs and humans, many of the successful rehabs we did and the work we still do with reactivity could not ever have happened and could not continue to happen. So I would like to pass on a massive thank you to all at CaDeLac, past and present, team members and clients, dogs and humans who have helped with the rehab of so many barking, lunging dogs. These dogs are now in educated, lifelong loving homes and not in rescue centres, **because of you! Thank you**!